The "Keystone" Jacket and Dress Cutter

An 1895 Guide to Women's Tailoring

Chas. Hecklinger

Preface to the Dover Edition by
Kristina Seleshanko7

Dover Publications, Inc.
Mineola, New York

Bibliographical Note

This Dover edition, first published in 2006, is an unabridged republication of *The "Keystone" Jacket and Dress Cutter*, published by The Herald of Fashion Co., New York, 1895. This volume also includes a new Preface to the Dover edition, plus additional illustrations reproduced from *The Delineator* magazine, June, 1895 and June, 1896. New captions have been provided for these illustrations.

Library of Congress Cataloging-in-Publication Data

Hecklinger, Charles.
     The "Keystone" jacket and dress cutter : an 1895 guide to women's tailoring / Chas. Hecklinger ; preface by Kristina Seleshanko.
        p. cm.
     Reprint. Originally published: New York : Herald of Fashion Co., 1895.
     ISBN-13: 978-0-486-45105-3 (pbk.)
     ISBN-10: 0-486-45105-4 (pbk.)
     1. Dressmaking—Pattern design. 2. Tailoring (Women's) I. Title.

TT520.H475 2006
646.4'0409034—dc22

                                                                                                2006040607

Manufactured in the United States by LSC Communications
4500050610
www.doverpublications.com

INDEX.

		PAGE
Title	-	1
Preface to the Dover Edition	-	5
Preface	-	7
Introduction	-	7
The Measures	-	8
Drafting the Waist	-	12
Large Form with Extra Length of Waist	-	18
Stout Form	-	20
Erect Form	-	22
Stooping Form	-	24
The Eton Jacket	-	26
The Bolero or Zouave Jacket	-	28
The Darts in the Forepart	-	29
The Dart for a Very Narrow Front	-	30
Darts for Small-waisted Forms	-	31
Low-neck Waist	-	32
Jackets	-	33
Jackets with Full Skirts	-	36
Short Jacket with Plaited Skirt	-	40
Cutaway Jackets	-	41
Covert Jacket	-	42
Frock Coat	-	44
Cutaway Frock Jacket	-	46
Riding Jacket, Double-breasted	-	48
Riding Jacket, Single-breasted	-	50
Shirt Waists	-	52
Shirt Waist with Yoke	-	54
The Plain Sleeve	-	56
Changes from the Plain Sleeve	-	58
Large Sleeve Head	-	60

	PAGE
A Very Full Sleeve	62
Sleeve for Shirt Waist	64
Single-breasted Vests	66
Double-breasted Vests	70
Collars	72
Broad Collars	75
Full Round Collar	76
Three-quarter Cape	76
Plain Cape	78
Wrap-shaped Cape	78
The Ulster	80
Dress Skirts	82
The Full Dress Skirt	84
Riding Skirt	86
Trousers	90
Breeches	92
Illustrations from *The Delineator*, June, 1895 and June, 1896e	95

PREFACE TO THE DOVER EDITION

THE 1890s were a time of exuberant and opulent fashions. Velvet, silk, satin, and taffeta were favored fabrics, while yards and yards of cloth were "necessary" for women's clothes. Stylish fashions called for bold colors—bright fuchsia, sunny yellow, cherry red, turquoise—and color combinations could be quite audacious. "Daring combinations are effected in colors," noted an editor for *The Delineator* magazine, "such as violet with mauve or green, pale-blue with the dull shades of green, and yellow with soft shades of gray." Magazines featured increasingly large hats, trimmed with an abundance of flowers and feathers—even whole birds! Ruffles and frills were in excess.

As portrayed in widely circulated magazines, the woman of the 1890s dressed vividly and had plenty of time to participate in boating, tennis, golf, and horseback riding. She was smart, well-educated, had a hearty sense of humor, and was curvy and robust. In short, she was the antithesis of the fashionable belle of her grandmother's generation, who was thin, fragile, and favored pale shades.

But there was a more subtle, sober side to the 1890s. Better educated, with more jobs open to them in the workforce, women pursued a more active lifestyle. As a result, the woman of the 1890s began developing a sort of daily uniform. It was practical (at least by the standards of the time), and not as attention-getting as most other feminine clothing. Almost every woman of the 1890s relied on tailored suits, with full skirts and fitted jackets buttoned over simple blouses or shirtwaists. Women wore this costume while on errands, in the office, or for traveling. They even wore a modified version during favorite outdoor pastimes—hiking, horseback riding, or bicycling.

Tailored suits for women were nothing new. Tailor-made riding habits had been popular for women since the end of the eighteenth century, and by the1860s, women's suits for everyday living began to appear regularly in fashion magazines. But it was when women began exploring their world more freely in the 1890s—whether by working outside the home or cycling around town—that the tailored suit became a staple of feminine attire.

There's little doubt that suits for women were more practical than the furbelowed, fussy styles otherwise worn, but tailored clothes were not exactly what moderns would call "no-nonsense," either. First, there was the comfort factor. Bodices were still tight and skirts still swept the streets. Author and artist Gwen Raverat complained especially of the long skirts of the era. "It was difficult to walk freely in the heavy tweed 'walking skirts,' which kept on catching between the knees," she wrote. "Round the bottom of these skirts I had, with my own hands, sewn two and a half yards of 'brush braid,' to collect the worst of the mud; for they inevitably sweep the roads, however carefully I might hold them up behind . . . Afterwards the crusted mud had to be brushed off, which might take an hour or more to do."

Garments also required a tremendous amount of labor and resources to create. The skirts Raverat complained about, for example, required about six yards of cloth. They were often stiffened, not just with a lining, but with cording sewn into the hem. The enormous sleeves of 1895 took about three and a half yards of fabric (apiece!), and were fully lined. In fact, the popular ladies' magazine *Demorest's* confessed that dressmakers exercised "ingenuity," so that "as many yards of material as possible can be gracefully arranged to fall from the shoulder."

Each piece of a woman's bodice was actually composed of two pieces: the outer cloth, and the lining. These were cut from the same pattern and basted together; then, the various pieces were seamed. Most bodice seams were boned, which required hand stitching. Shirtwaists and suits fastened in the front with hooks and eyes (all hand sewn in place and sometimes topped with decorative buttons) or with functional buttons and hand-stitched buttonholes. The high collars of the 1890s were either boned or interlined with stiff cloth.

The simplest tailored item a woman owned was a shirtwaist, and it was rarely "plain." Many women considered the shirtwaist, although covered with pleats, tucks, smocking, and gathering, the ultimate in practicality. "I think the most important inventions of the century are the bicycle and the shirtwaist," said one young woman to Victorian author Alexander Black. "Each has had an important influence on the physical and economic situation of women." Highly versatile and far more comfortable than the fitted bodices of the period, the shirtwaist was probably the most popular fashion of the 1890s.

The Eton jacket, first introduced to women's fashions in the 1890s, and based on the mid-nineteenth-century blazers worn by boys at Eton College, continued to be essential to female attire. A comeback from women's Civil War-era fashions, Zouave (or bolero) jackets with collarless necks and short waists and sleeves, were also commonly found in women's wardrobes. In addition, most women owned several detachable collars and at least one vest—a style deftly stolen from men's fashions and made undoubtedly feminine simply by hugging feminine curves.

And then there was the riding habit. Begun as an over-jacket (called a "redingote") in the late eighteenth century, this relatively minor garment worn by the elite was turned by the Victorians into an elaborate getup worn by almost all female riders. Consisting of a snugly fitted bodice with long sleeves and a high collar, a pair of trousers, and a long draped skirt, worn with high boots and a veiled hat, the riding habit was possibly the most expensive tailored garment a woman could buy. Riding habits were also one of the main reasons books like *The "Keystone" Jacket and Dress Cutter* were highly popular among professional tailors. Such books not only offered detailed patterns for oddly shaped riding skirts, they helped tailors navigate newer styles . . . and customer relations. For example, any embarrassment a Victorian woman (or tailor) might feel at an ordinary suit fitting was intensified when making elaborate riding skirts and pants. As the author of *The Cutter's Practical Guide* (a tailoring manual of the early 1900s) maintained: "The cutter must be careful to shew [sic] every possible respect to the customer, and then, as long as he goes about his business in a business-like manner, no lady will object to any adjustment that is necessary for the success of the garment."

Thus, by offering masculine tailors a guide to the world of feminine attire, books like *"Keystone"* carefully paved the way for women to explore their world in a more practical—and yes, fashionable—way.

KRISTINA SELESHANKO

PREFACE.

IN preparing this work an endeavor has been made to do three things : First, to make the systems the simplest and most reliable ever offered to the trade ; second, to illustrate and explain them so clearly and fully that to study and not understand them will be impossible ; and third, to consider and exhaustively treat every style of garment made for women by tailors and dressmakers. That the success attained may be considered commensurate with the intention, study and labor the work represents, is the earnest hope of the

AUTHOR.

INTRODUCTION.

RECOGNIZING the great and growing need of a reliable and comprehensive text book on ladies' tailoring, and in response to the innumerable inquiries for such a work that have come to the writer during the past few years, the systems and technical information given in these pages were made and compiled. The systems are the outgrowth of the practical experience of the author and of many others who are expert in ladies' tailoring, and combine simplicity and accuracy as they were never before combined in the systematic delineation of ladies' garments.

They are essentially the same as those published by the same author some years ago, the principles of which have been demonstrated to be sound by severe and long continued tests under every variety of condition ; but they have been so improved as scarcely to be recognized and are, for all practical purposes, new systems. That this work contains a larger amount of valuable information about ladies' tailoring than is contained in all other works on the subject ever published, will be cheerfully admitted, we are sure, by any one who carefully studies it.

THE MEASURES.

THE greatest possible care should be taken in measuring to obtain correct lengths and widths, as only right measures will enable us, in drafting, to define the size and position or attitude of the form measured.

We must, therefore, take the measures from and to accurately located points.

The height of the neck can be easily and correctly located by the eye, and the front and bottom of the arm by the use of a small square ; but the waist line, which is a measuring station of the greatest importance, must be defined as follows :

Place an elastic band around the waist, just above the hips, and adjust it so that it is perfectly level.

Whether the waist is to be long or short, the band must be placed as directed ; the actual waist length can then be increased or diminished according to style or taste.

As the measures that terminate at the belt govern the balance of the garment and indicate attitude, the importance of adjusting it accurately *and always over the same part of the waist will be apparent.*

Having adjusted the belt, proceed as follows :

THE BACK LENGTH.

Apply the measuring tape to the socket bone at the neck as marked by A, Figure 1, and measure down to the lower edge of the belt, which gives the actual length of the back.

Should we desire to make the waist longer or make it appear so, because taste or style requires it, take what extra length may be suggested before removing the tape from the neck.

For a jacket we continue down to the point where the bottom should be, and for a long ulster, to the floor, as to D and E.

FRONT LENGTH.

Placing the tape to the same point at neck, carry it along the neck, and let it fall over the shoulder past the front of the arm. It should not be drawn down close against the arm but should pass from 1 to 1½ inch in front of it, but not over the bust, straight down to the bottom of the belt at the side, as shown on Figure 2, where the point is marked N.

THE FRONT OF ARM.

This is also called the " Blade Measure." For this we use a small square with a short tape measure attached.

This square is placed under the arm, against which, as it hangs straight down, it presses firmly.

The tape is then drawn smoothly across to the center of the back, at B, as shown on Figure 1, and the measure noted.

FIGURE 1.   FIGURE 2.

THE HEIGHT UNDER ARM.

Without removing the square draw the tape downward, being careful not to disturb or lower the square, and measure to the bottom of the belt at G.

Should the square have changed its position, replace it close up to the arm again.

THE LENGTH OF SLEEVE.

While the square is in position draw the tape down straight to the wrist at K, or to the point desired for the length of the sleeve.

This ends the usefulness of the square.

THE BREAST MEASURE.

Standing behind the figure we place the tape across the fullest part of breast and carry it under the arms and across the back, being careful that it adheres over the surface closely, and call off the measure. This should be smoothly taken, neither too close nor too easy.

THE WAIST MEASURE.

Remove the elastic belt, and place the tape around the waist and draw it tight. Should a belt be worn it had better be removed, especially when measuring for a dress-waist. In the latter case take the size very close.

THE HIP MEASURE

Is taken 6 inches below the natural waist, always easy, and smoothly around. No measure is required below the hips.

THE ELBOW.

The elbow measure is taken close to obtain the size of arm. Any width can easily be added over this for easy sleeves.

THE WRIST.

Around the cuff of dress or wrist, also taken close to obtain the right size, any extra size needed is added.

On button-up dresses take a close neck measure.

THE SYSTEM.

DRAFTING THE WAIST.

DIAGRAM 1.

I SHALL commence to explain the drafting of ladies' garments by showing first how a waist pattern is produced.

This being the covering for the body, from the neck down to the natural waist its construction gives the principle on which all close-fitting garments are based. Whatever the shape or measures used, the points are all established on this principle; and this, therefore, will be the foundation of all our drafts.

We shall use the following measures to draft by:

Back length to natural waist, - - -	15 inches.
Front length to side of hip, - - -	18½ "
The blade, or front of arm, - - - -	10 "
The height under the arm, - - -	7½ "
Breast, - - - - - -	36 "
Waist, - - - - - -	24 "

Begin by drawing the line O B, and at a right angle with this draw the line O F.

From O to 1 place ¾ inch. *This is always the same, whether the measure is small or large.*

From 1, which will be the top of back, apply the natural waist length, which is 15 inches, giving point B.

Upward from B place the height under the arm, 7½ inches in this case, giving point A. Now square lines across from A and B.

From B to C is $\frac{1}{12}$ of the breast size. Draw a line from C to 1 at top of back, and from where this line crosses the breast line at A1, apply one-half the breast measure, 18 inches, to locate G.

From A1—the back seam—measure out the "Front of Arm" measure to K. This is 10 inches. At K square a line up and down, as shown to I and J.

Now, on the long arm of the square, we find what size is given on the Two-Thirds *scale opposite the 10-inch (size of blade) point. Having ascertained what it is—for this size it is 15, or ½ of 30—we find on the short arm 15 on the Scale of Fourths— 3¾ inches —and this amount we place back from K to obtain L, from where a line is drawn up to the top line.*

Divide the distance between the top—V—and the under-arm line in halves, which gives point Z.

Point T is half-way between Z and the top line, point V.

In the middle, between T and Z, is point 3.

From O to 2 is ⅛ of the blade, 15, the amount found as explained above in italics. Connect 2 with 3 by a straight line, and curve the top of the back from 1 to 2.

O to 9 is ⅓ of the breast, 6 inches. Square a line down from 9. Opposite Z is 8 on the line just drawn.

From X to C draw a straight guide line. Make the width of the bottom of the back, C to D, 1½ inch and form the back.

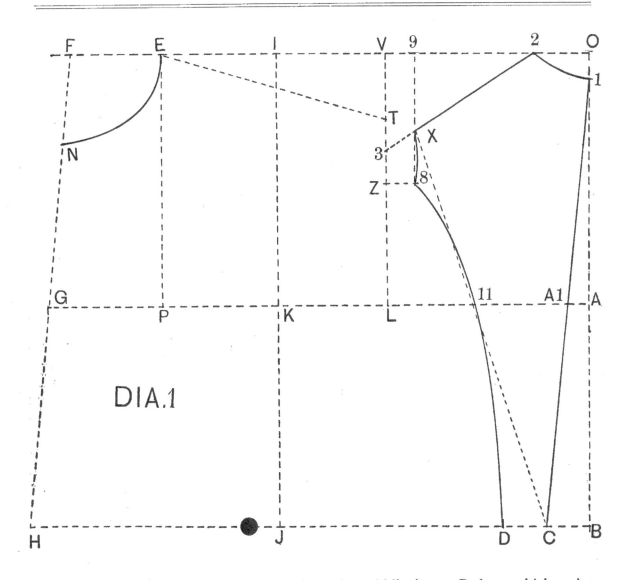

DIA.1

Measure the distance G to K, and in the middle locate P, from which point square up to E on the top line.

To locate the front length in accordance with the measure, apply the tape 1 inch in front of J on the waist line, as at the dot, and measure up to E, the front length, 18½ inches, *less the width of the top of back.* This will place point E on the upper line in this case.

But this measure will vary for erect and stooping forms. For erect forms it will reach above the upper line, as on Diagrams 6 and 7, and then a line is drawn to the front as E to F, from which point the neck is formed.

For stooping figures this measure is short and will not reach to the top line, as seen on Diagram 8, where it is fully explained.

E is the front shoulder point. Now draw a straight line from E to T.

Place from E to F ⅙ of the breast measure, and to N the same from F down.

Next draw a straight line for the run of the front from F down through G, reaching H.

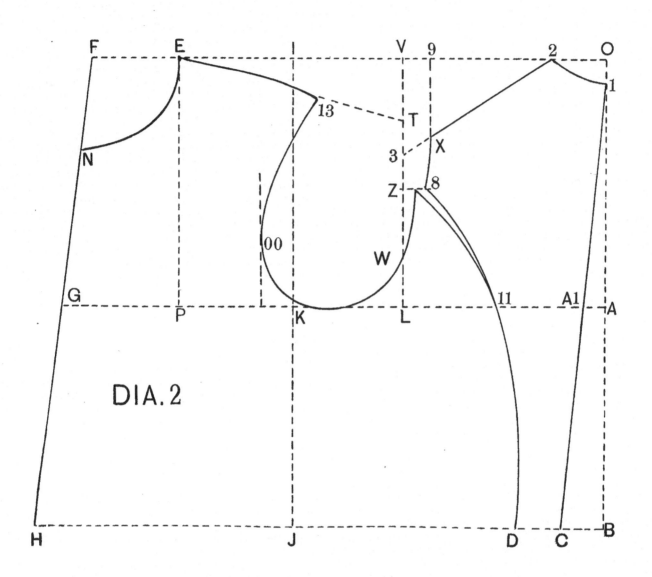

DIAGRAM 2.

Take the distance of back-shoulder from 2 to X, place it on the line from E to 13, and curve the front shoulder slightly.

The distance between the lines X and 3 is placed forward of line K, giving line O O.

Form the arm-hole from 13 to O O and K.

Go in from 8 to top of sidebody ¼ inch ; curve the side-seam from 11 up, and finish the arm-hole, being careful not to curve too much at W.

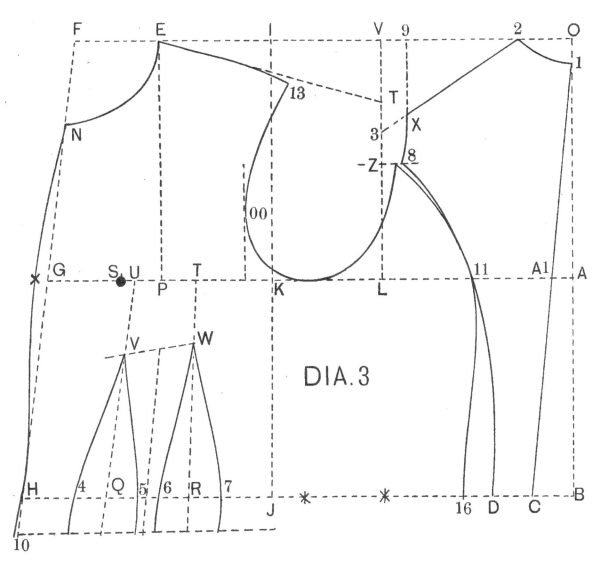

DIAGRAM 3.

From D to 16 is 1 inch.

The sidebody seam is now drawn from 11 down to 16, with a slight round.

Go out from G to the front line ½ inch and shape the front from N, passing the star near G, and touching at H.

Divide the distance G—K into 3 parts, which gives S and T.

Place point U ½ inch back of S.

Divide the distance H and J into 3 parts, giving points Q and R.

Draw lines from U through Q and from T through R, for the center of the darts.

Make V ⅓ from U to Q, and make W ½ inch higher.

Measure the pattern from C to D and 16 to H, which will be found to be 17 inches, an amount much too great for the size of the waist.

The amount *that it is too large* must be taken out in darts, two of which we take out on every waist.

The size of the pattern is 17 inches.

Pattern, - - - - - -	17 inches.
½ waist, - - - - - -	12 inches.
Difference, - - - - -	5 inches.

We add a cut under arm of ½ inch, which amount is to be taken from this 5 inches, leaving 4½ inches for the darts. This gives us 2¼ inches for each dart, which amount is placed equally on each side of the center lines Q and R.

From Q, therefore, to 4 and 5 is 1⅛ inch, and from R to 6 and 7 is also 1⅛ inch.

Now draw the darts.

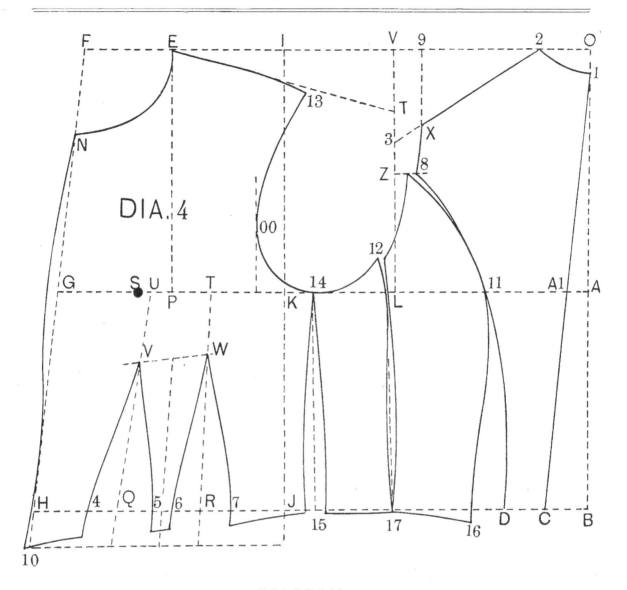

DIAGRAM 4.

On this diagram take the distance from the dart at 7 to 16, and divide it into 3 parts, giving points 15 and 17.

From point 15 draw a straight line up to 14, parallel with that from J to K.

From point 17 draw the line so that it will be nearly parallel with line 14 to 15.

But it may be desirable to obtain a sidebody narrow at the arm-hole; if it is, place the line closer to the back.

At 12 nip a slight amount from the middle sidebody, but let the upper point remain on the same level, so that one seam will not be shorter than the other.

Curve the seam slightly below L by taking out no more than ¼ inch.

On the seam 14 to 15 we must take out ½ inch at 15—the amount we subtracted from the total waist when regulating the darts.

Add to the front length from H to 10 1 inch, and shape bottom edge from 16, which is ½ below the waist line, to 17, on to 15 and forward to 10.

LARGE FORM WITH EXTRA LENGTH OF WAIST.

DIAGRAM 5.

THE measures by which this diagram was drafted are as follows :

Waist length,	15–20½.
Front length,	18½.
Blade-measure,	10¾.
Height under arm,	7½.
Breast,	40.
Waist,	28.
Hip,	46.

Draw all the lines and establish all the points in the same manner as already explained, with the following exceptions :

The pattern measures from C to D and 16 to H, 19½ inches, while the waist is only 14 inches.

Pattern,	19½ inches.
Waist,	14 inches.
Difference,	5½ inches.

Taking off ¼ inch for the cut under the arm leaves us 5 inches to be divided and applied to the two darts, or 2½ inches to each.

This is applied equally on each side of the center lines Q and R.

To give the darts a good shape, draw a line in the middle between V and W and 5 and 6, and make the seams run below 5 and 6 to 2 and 3, with only a perceptible difference in width at 2 and 3 beyond that at 5 and 6.

From 4 on the waist line the seam is straight to 1, but from 7 to O it springs out nearly, or quite, to the straight center line of dart.

After the under-arm seams have been established, draw a line across 6 inches below the waist line for the hip.

Draw a line from the top of the sidebody through point 16 at waist, and curve below 16 somewhat for round of hip, or about ½ inch from E to 9.

Draw a straight guide line from C down at right angles with the waist line, then extend the back-seam line down from C, so that it will be in the middle between the two dotted lines and reach to F.

From D draw the line straight down square with the waist-line.

Next to establish the spring needed for hip room according to the measures, we first measure F to E, then 9 to O, then 3 to 2, and then 1 to front line M.

This gives us 19 inches, while ½ of the hip is 23 inches.

Hip,	23 inches.
Pattern,	19 inches.
Difference,	4 inches.

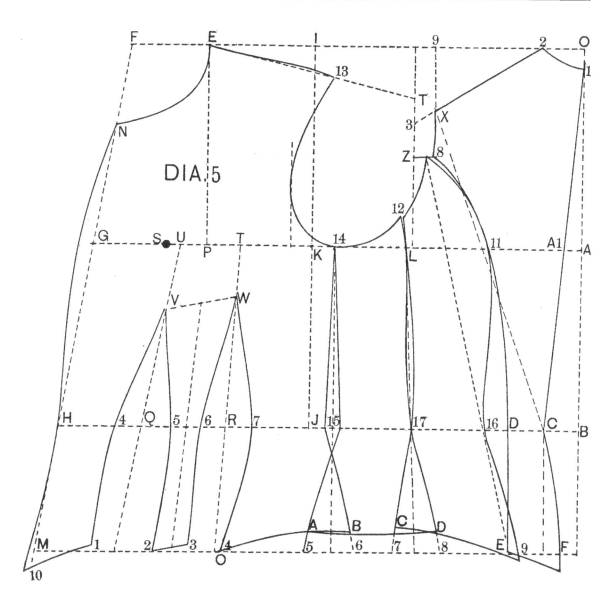

These 4 inches must be added to make the draft roomy enough to cover the hips.

The lines under the arms having been drawn as far as necessary, we place on either side of them to C and D 1 inch, and the same to A and B, making the allowance at each place 2 inches, or equal to the size we must have.

Commencing then at 17, draw to C and D, and commencing at 15 draw to A and B.

The lower edge may be drawn as on this diagram by shortening it over the hips, or it may remain on the lower straight line.

"*Remember in getting the size of the hips not to include the darts, as they are established and their amount is to be cut out.*"

STOUT FORM.

DIAGRAM 6.

THE measures for this diagram are :

Length of back,	-	-	-	-	-		15–19½.
Front length,	-	-	-	-	-	-	20.
Blade,	-	-	-	-	-	-	13.
Height under the arm,	-	-	-	-	-	-	7.
Breast,	-	-	-	-	-	-	46.
Waist,	-	-	-	-	-	-	33.

Obtain all the points by the measures as explained, with the following exceptions :

Mark a point 1 inch in front of J on the waist line.

Measure up from this point to the line at E, applying the front length 20, less the width of the top of the back. This measure locates point E somewhat above the top line, in this case 1 inch. It may, however, be more or less on different forms, as much in fact as 2 inches for very stout figures.

When point E has been established, draw a line over to F and place ⅙ of breast to locate F.

Then ⅙ breast is placed below F for the neck or height of gorge.

The neck in front is always regulated by the position of the shoulder point, and rises or falls with it.

On large forms, such as we are now considering, the distance between the darts and the back is so great that it is advisable to make three sidebodies.

Take the distance between the dart point 7 and the point of the sidebody at 16 and divide this in the middle, which gives B.

Then divide 7 and B, fixing 15, and also B and 16, locating 17.

Draw the first two lines, 14 to 15 and A to B, straight up, and that from 17 to 12 with the view of gaining a narrow form at top. Draw the seams by curving slightly, as suggested by the diagram.

The hip room is in this case divided on the three seams, each one being increased, of course, less than when there are only two used.

Should the form be very fleshy over the stomach, it will be necessary to add a trifle extra spring to the dart-seams below the waist line, as shown by 1, 2 and 3.

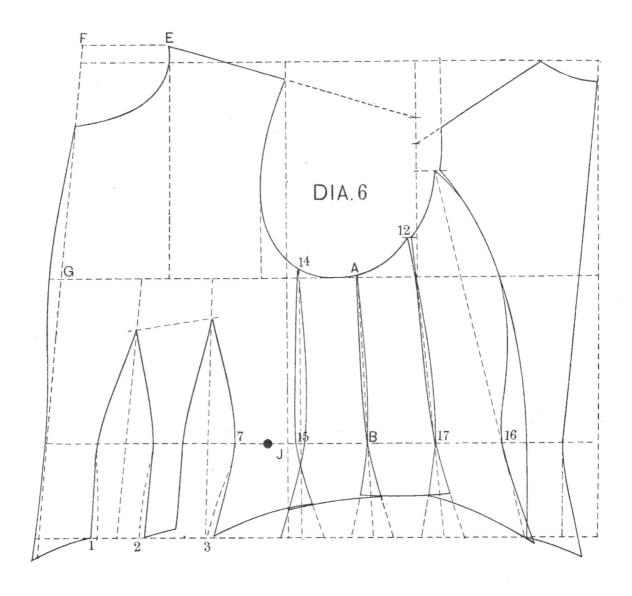

DIA. 6

ERECT FORM.

DIAGRAM 7.

THE measures of this draft are :

Length of back,	-	-	-	-	16–20.
Length of front,	-	-	-	-	21.
Blade measure,	-	-	-	-	10½.
Height under arm,	-	-	-	-	8.
Breast,	-	-	-	-	38.
Waist, -	-	-	-	-	26.
Hip, -	-	-	-	-	44.

All the points are located as already explained, with the following exceptions :

To establish the front shoulder apply the front length from the dot at side to line at E.   This will reach above the top line.

Always deduct from this measure the width of the top of back.

When E has been located, draw the line over to F, and place ⅙ of breast forward from E to fix F.

From F go down ⅙ breast to N for the neck, and draw all the other lines as directed.

It will be seen that the lower edge is kept straight across the hip line, the same as on a short jacket.

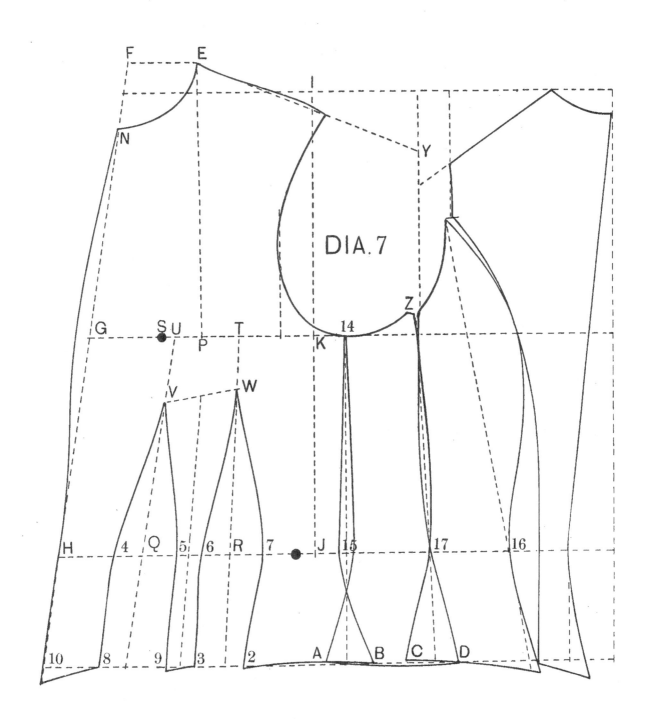

DIA. 7

STOOPING FORM.

DIAGRAM 8.

FOR this form the measures are :

Length of back,	-	-	-	-	-	16–18.
Front length,	-	-	-	-	-	18½.
Blade,	-	-	-	-	-	10½.
Height under arm,	-	-	-	-	-	7½.
Breast,	-	-	-	-	-	36.
Waist,	-	-	-	-	-	25.

The points are located by these measures as previously explained, with the following exceptions :

In drawing in the darts, guide lines may be of benefit. These are as follows :

After the points have been located, draw straight lines from V through 4 and 5, and from W through 6 and 7.

It will be seen that from 4 down to 8 the dart-seam must run nearly straight down, and that those from 5 to 9 and 6 to 3 follow with the same shape. The one from 7 to 2, however, must have more spring, or twice as much from the dotted line as any of the others.

The front length in this case is short because of the stooping figure and flatness of chest.

Applying the front length, 18½ inches, toward E, it will not reach to the top line, but falls, instead, 1 inch below it.

When fixed, place over from 12 to F, on a line drawn from 12, the usual ⅙ breast, and from F to N the same.

Whenever the shoulder point is low the neck must follow.

As stooping forms usually have prominent shoulder-blades, it is necessary to enlarge slightly the opening between the top of the sidebody and the back at 8, and take out at waist (16) ¼ to ⅜ inch more to conform with the curve of the blade, and at the same time to enlarge the opening at Z a trifle.

It is also an advantage to take a measure from the neck in front, N, to the natural waist, to determine how long the front should be.

A form like the one just described needs no change in the darts.

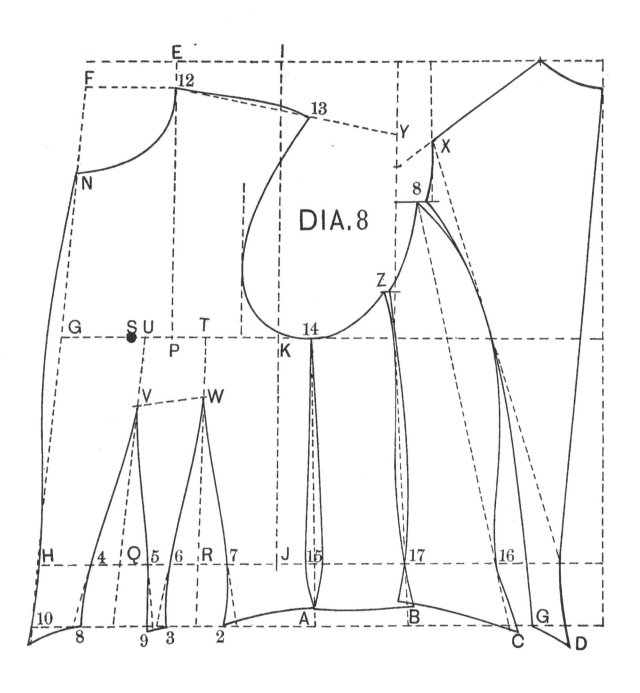

THE ETON JACKET.

DIAGRAM 9.

AFTER the right-angled lines O F and O B have been drawn, place from O to 1 the regular ¾ inch.

From 1 to B is the length of the natural waist.

B up to A the height under the arm.

The other fitting points are all fixed by the measures, as already explained.

When point X has been established, lay the square against the back line A1 and D, and move it up or down till its short arm will rest on point X, and then draw a line to X.

Next place the square on this line and square down from X to 8, giving thus the best run of the scye line of the back.

This method can be used on all drafts, instead of merely relying on the eye.

Only one dart is needed and cut in these jackets, and we must therefore reduce the size one-third at the side under the arm, leaving only two-thirds for the dart as the amount to be suppressed to the size of the waist.

In locating the one dart, start it from the center point P and let the line run parallel with the front edge, which causes the distance Q H to be equal to that of P to G, and then place what is to be taken out in a dart on either side of Q to 5 and 6.

Do not curve the lines of the dart below the waist line, but follow the form shown at S and T. This will cause the jacket to cling close to the waist, while if spring were added it would be loose on the lower edge and flare out.

The shape at the bottom is 1 to 1½ inch longer than the natural waist at back, point 10, and only ½ to ¾ inch over the hips; but toward the front it points downward, giving the effect desired.

The star below the shoulder point E is 1 inch from the curve of the neck.

From this point the break line is drawn to where the roll is to turn, and the turn of the lapel is added beyond this — made wide or slim as individual taste may desire.

These jackets have a peaked lapel and narrow coat collar. The latter is usually drafted like the one shown by Diagram 63, but that shown by Diagram 60 will answer equally as well.

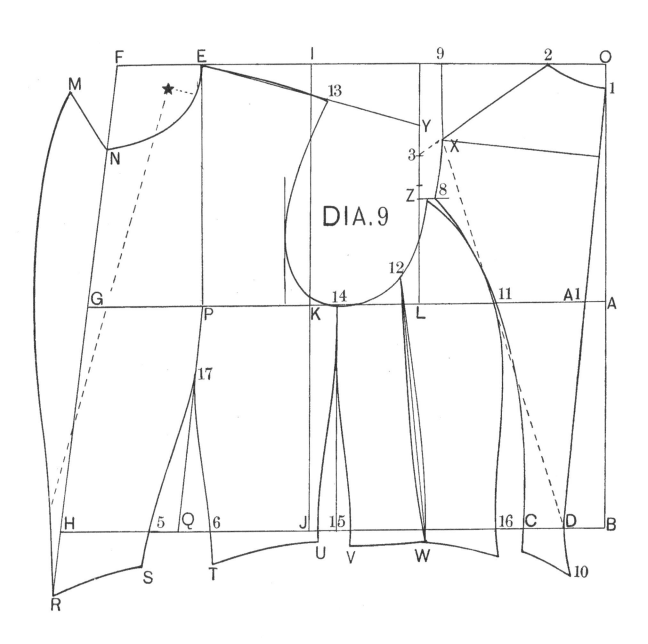

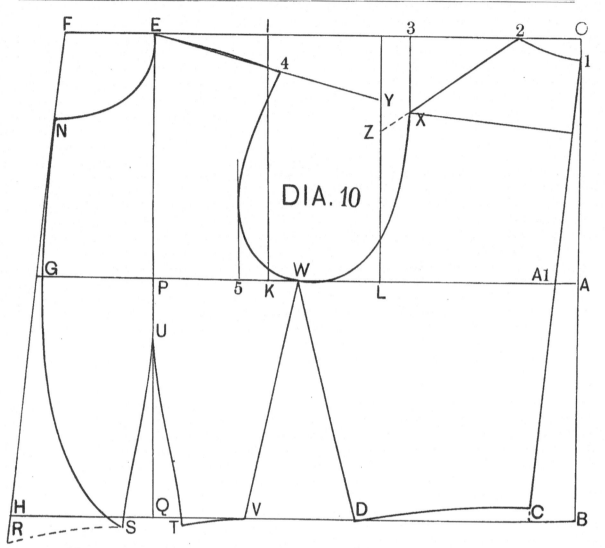

THE BOLERO, OR ZOUAVE JACKET.

DIAGRAM 10.

DRAW the lines O B and O F. From O to 1 is ¾ inch. From 1 to B is the waist length.

Up from B to A is the height under the arm. The widths are fixed as for any waist. When the front edge is established, take the middle between G and A1, which fixes W. Draw the dart line straight down from point P, and make the width from S to T only ⅓ of what the darts demand.

Place ¼ waist from C to D, and make the distance from front line H to S and T to V the same. Connect W with V by a straight line, and also W with D. The front is either shaped like the diagram, or made pointed at the bottom of the front.

These jackets are often made from 1 to 2 inches shorter than the natural waist line, but when so made no dart is taken out, because they must be loose around the bottom. No collar is required. If a revere is to be added it is the same as for a jacket.

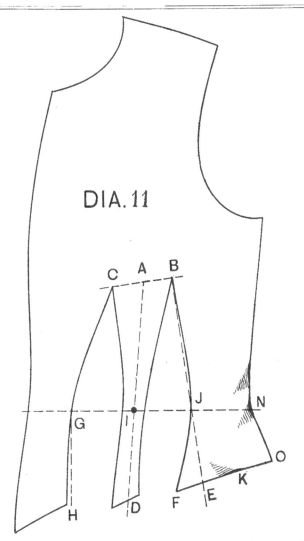

DIA. 11

THE DARTS IN THE FOREPART.

DIAGRAM 11.

THE location of the darts and the way the seam lines are drawn exert considerable influence on the fit of the front.

If they have been drawn to the size required, and are shaped as those on this diagram, they will be just right. But that no mistake may occur, we suggest the use of guide lines In the middle between the tops of the darts, points C and B, we have located A, and in the middle of the center-piece at I we have made a dot.

From A through this dot draw a straight line like the one shown. Now the width of the center piece should be equal on each side of the straight line, and should be for 2 to 3 inches below the waist line no greater in width than at I on the waist line. It will be seen, therefore, that both of these seam lines are straight down from the waist, but the one from G is a trifle more forward.

With the view of gaining some spring at the bottom at K and at the side at N, it is desirable to shape the line from J to F to about 1½ inch from the straight line E from B through J. This is better than to add spring at the side, O, for this would produce wrinkles at the waist.

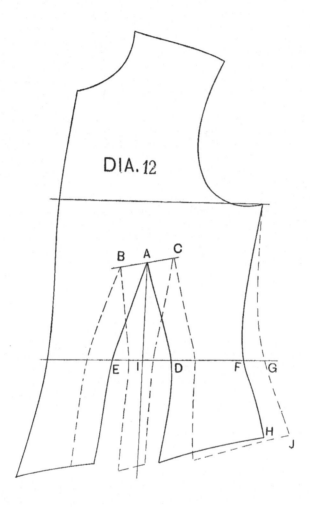

DIAGRAM 12.

On very narrow fronts it may be advisable to take out only one dart, which is here illustrated.

First both darts are drawn to the size required. Then in the middle, A through I, we draw a line and place on each side to E and D ⅔ of both darts, and shape the seams below the waist line as shown.

The ⅓ that is left is taken off the side from G to F, and the side-seam is then formed as represented.

Be sure that the front and also the back line of the dart will retain the same shape as the original darts as shown by the dotted lines.

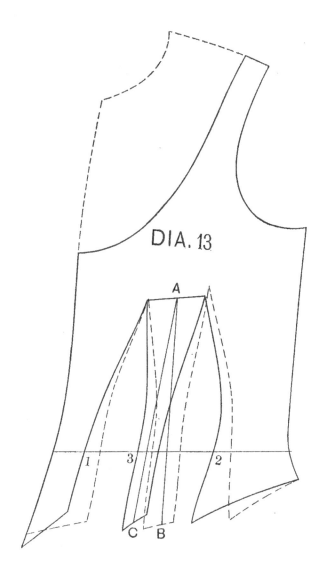

DIAGRAM 13.

On all small-waisted forms, or on dress waists, transferring the front dart forward 1 inch at 1, as shown by the solid line, will give the waist more of a pointed appearance toward the bottom, and cause it to appear narrow in front.

The size of the first dart is, therefore, drawn in from 1 to 3, and the piece between the darts is retained of the same width; the second dart is then drawn to the original width.

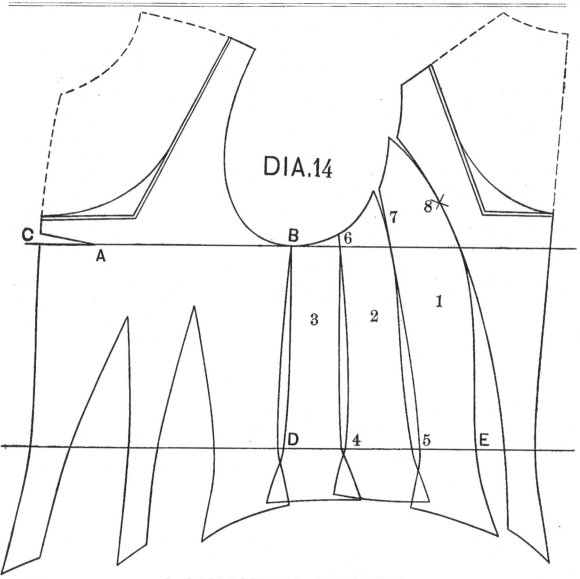

LOW-NECK WAIST.
DIAGRAM 14.

THIS is drawn to measure.   It is then cut down on the back and the front to a
square shape, reaching to within 2 inches of the breast line.

A V at the front of breast, ¼ inch wide, is usually taken out from C to A.
This V is cut only in the lining, and the outside material must be arranged over it.

The darts are always advanced, as explained for Diagram 13.

All dress waists require 3 sidebodies, in order that no one shall be wider at the
waist than another, as narrow sidebodies facilitate the work in obtaining a smooth
fit about the waist line.

To have these in equal proportion, take the distance from the inside edge
of the last dart to E, divide it into 4 equal parts, giving points D, 4 and 5, and
draw the seams as shown.

Those from D to B and 4 to 6 run straight up, but that from 5 and 7 is drawn
so that the last sidebody between 7 and 8 will appear narrow.

The low-neck effect is also drawn on a curve so as to show two styles.

JACKETS.

DIAGRAM 15.

TO show the best way of drafting these, so that it may be clearly understood, we shall go over every point in the most careful manner.

The measures to be used are :

The back length to the natural waist, - - -	15.
Total length to the bottom, - - -	32.
Front length to the side of hip, - - - -	19.
The blade, or front of arm, - - -	10.
The height under the arm, - - - -	7½.
Breast, - - - - - - -	36.
Waist, - - - - - - -	25.
Hip, - - - - - -	46.

It may be the place just here to state that all jackets of sack shape are drafted in a similar manner to this one, and that the length alters in no way the location of the points or the run of the lines.

While this example is drafted with two darts, others are given where only one is used, or none at all, and by following the instructions given every modification can readily be adopted.

HOW TO DRAFT.

First we draw the line from O to C, and the one at top from O to T at a right angle with the first line.

From O to 1 is ¾ inch for the top of back.

Apply the waist length from 1 to the waist line at B, 16 inches, and continue down to the bottom at C, 32 inches, the full length.

Go up from B to fix A, the height under the arm, which is 7½ inches.

Now, from points A, B and C, draw square lines across.

From B to D is $\frac{1}{12}$ of breast.

Draw the back-seam from 1 to D.

Make the width of back at waist from D to 6 about 1½ inch for a short jacket, and a trifle more for a long one.

At a right angle with the waist line draw one down from D, which reaches the point marked ⅞, and also draw one down from 6, which reaches the point marked ⅝.

Extend the back line down from D to C, giving it a slight outward curve.

Whatever has been added at the bottom from ⅞ to C must be placed from ⅝ to 10, to give the run of the side-seam from 6 at waist to point 10 at bottom.

Place from the back-seam, A1, to H, the blade measure, 10 inches, and draw a line up and down to V and J.

The distance to H being 10 inches, ⅔ is 15, or ½ of 30.

We bear in mind the number 15, and seek on the short arm the fourth of the same, which is equivalent to 3¾ inches, and place this back from H to give point F.

From F up to the top line draw a line square with that of the under-arm line.

Divide the distance between F and the top line, which gives point M, and also divide the distance of M and the top line, giving K.

In the middle between M and K place L.

Make the width of the top of the back from O to 2, ⅛ of the blade 15, and connect 2 with L by a straight line.

Go out from O along the top line to locate N, ⅓ of the breast, and draw a short line down to 4.

Make a mark opposite M at 4, and draw the side-seam of the back to 6.

Go in from 6 to 7 in all cases 1 inch, and nip in the top of the sidebody at 4 about ⅜ inch; then draw the sidebody from the latter point with a sharp curve to 7.

Lay a straight edge at 7 and the top of the sidebody, draw a line as shown by the dotted line on the diagram, which reaches to C, and then curve the seam over the hip line about ½ inch, as shown.

Curve the arm-hole from 5 to 4 and to the line under the arm, at point H.

Place from A1 to G ½ of the full breast measure for the front line.

In the middle between G and H at the arm-hole fix point P, from which a line is drawn up to the top.

Take the front length and apply it from the dot, which is 1 inch in front of point J at the waist, upward on the line P U, deducting from it the width of the top of the back.

This measure locates point U.

From U to point K draw a straight line, and place from U to 3 the width of the back shoulder, 2 to 5.

The distance between the lines 5 and K is placed from line H to fix line Oo.

Shape the arm-hole from 3 to H, touching line Oo.

From U to T place ⅙ of the breast, and from T through G draw the front line, which will reach to S.

Then curve beyond G ½ inch to Q, and below add ½ over R and straight down to the bottom, as shown by the solid line.

Go down from T ⅙ breast to 1 and form the neck.

Now we come to the darts.

Take the distance between H and G and divide it into 3 parts, which gives W and the dot in front of X.

Make a mark ½ inch back of the dot, which will be X.

Next measure the distance between Q and J and divide this into 3 parts, giving the two stars numbered ¼ and ½.

From X and W draw straight lines through the stars down to the bottom.

To find out what must be taken out in darts, we measure the size of the pattern from D to 6 and 7 to Q, which in this case gives 17 inches.

Deducting the ½ size of the waist, 13 inches, from 17, leaves 4 inches, which is the amount for the darts, and as there are two of them, each will be 2 inches wide.

Place, then, from the star at ¼ to U and V 1 inch, and from the star at ½ to Y and X, also 1 inch, which will make each V 2 inches wide.

A little higher than ½ from the waist line to that under arm locate 3 and Z. Shape the seams of the darts through U V, X and Y, and continue the lines down to 12 and 13, where they will be about ½ inch apart.

Where these lines pass the hips, give them a slight curve toward the center line.

Measure the distance from the dart at Y to 7 and divide into 3 parts, giving 9 and 8.

From 9 draw a straight line up and down parallel to the line J H.

From 8 a straight line is also drawn up and down.

Curve and take out on line 9 about ½ inch and only a trifle on seam 8.

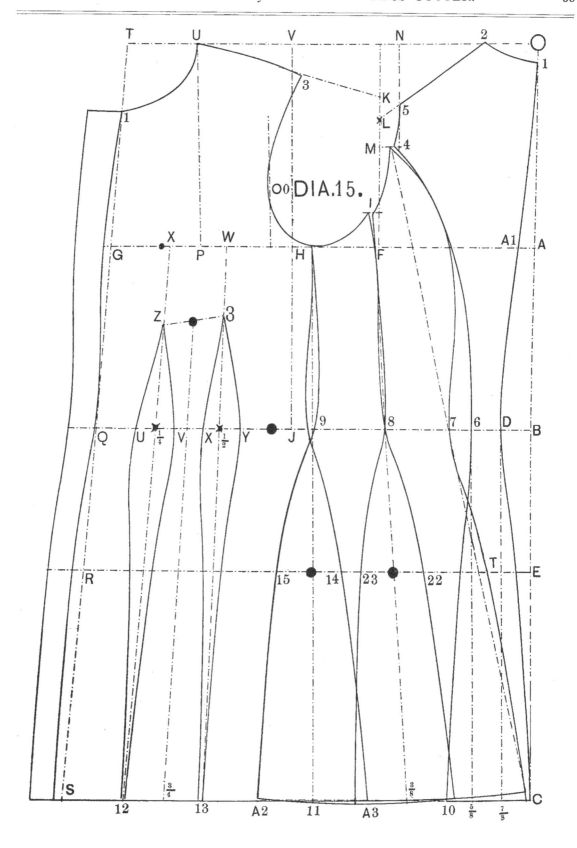

DIA.15.

Now we must add the hip room, and in getting this we first measure the width of the back on the line E, which is 6 inches below the waist line.

Then measure from the sidebody at T to the front at R, deducting the size of the darts, which gives 19 inches.

But one-half hip calls for 23 inches, which requires 4 inches to be added. These 4 inches we place on each side of the black dots on the hip line, 1 inch each to 15–14 and 23–22, and then draw the seams, curving from 9 and 8 through these points to the bottom.

The utmost care is to be taken that all lines below the waist shall run parallel to each other, except those on the back.

We have seen that the back line of the sidebody from 7 to C is regulated by the line from top to C.

Now the one from 8 to 10 should be equi-distant all the way down, so that 10 to C will be the same distance as 22 to T, and so all the others.

It will be noticed that all lines tending backward are parallel with the first line, 7 to C, and all those forward follow the shape of the line from Q to S.

Add 1 inch in front of the line 1 Q for lap for a single-breasted front.

As the lines below the waist overlap it is difficult to cut the pieces out, as all require piecing.

To obviate this, underlay the draft by a sheet of paper, and with a tracing wheel trace along the line of the sidebody 4, 7 to C and I, 8 to A3.

This gives you the sidebody next to the back.

It will be of advantage in regulating the length to mark the waist line.

Cut out the sidebody.

Then, having a sheet of paper underneath the other sidebody, we trace it out along the lines H, 9 to A 2, and I, 8 to 10, also tracing the waist line.

We now have the two sidebodies, and can proceed to cut out the back and the front. In doing this, we destroy the two sidebodies, but by tracing them we have them in full size, and thus have also been enabled to get the back and the front without piecing.

JACKETS WITH FULL SKIRTS.

DIAGRAMS 16, 17, 18 AND 19.

DIAGRAM 16.—The jacket drafted, as illustrated and explained for Diagram 15, is to measure, and will therefore cling close to the figure over the hips.

To produce the skirt part with a certain amount of drapery, some addition is required over the pattern as drawn.

It is not necessary to draw a new pattern to obtain the extra fullness that may be desired, as it can be marked out directly on the cloth.

Yet when it occurs that the amount of material is scant, it will be advisable to have a correct pattern.

We take the back first (see Diagram 16), mark along its edges down to the waist, and one inch below the waist line mark another line as B, and 6 inches below another as C.

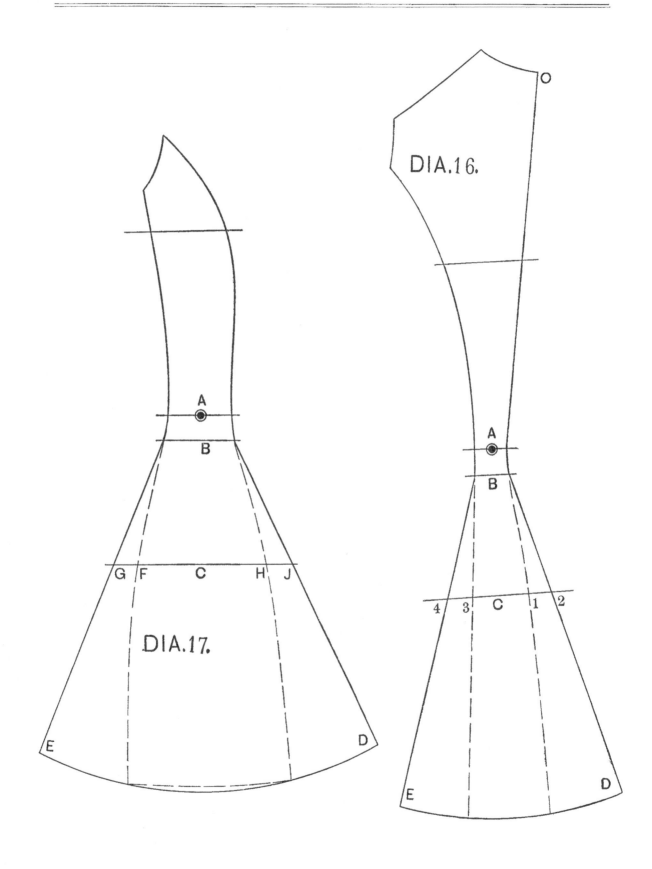

DIA.16.

DIA.17.

The original pattern is represented by the dotted lines.

Now for a full-skirted coat that will show considerable fullness below the waist, add 1 inch from 3 to 4, and the same from 1 to 2.

Then draw straight lines from the edge of the pattern on line B through 2 and 4, which will reach D and E.

Mark a point in the middle of waist as A, and pivoting at this point sweep the bottom each way to gain the right length.

DIAGRAM 17.—The first sidebody is marked along the edges down to the waist.

One inch below this a line is drawn as marked by B, and 6 inches farther down is drawn the line C.

On each side of the original pattern from F to G and H to J place 1 inch, and then draw straight lines from the sides of the pattern on line B through J and G, which will reach E and D.

The center A is used as a pivot to sweep the bottom.

DIAGRAM 18.—Mark from the waist line up as shown. The same 1 inch is placed below A to B, and the hip line is 6 inches from A.

From F to G place 1 inch, and from D to E the same amount. Draw straight lines from line B through points G and E, which will reach to J and H.

From the center A sweep the lower edge.

THE FRONT DIAGRAM 19.

Mark along the pattern above the waist, down the front and the darts.

Place on line C, which is the same as on the other diagrams, 1 inch for extra hip, and draw from B a straight line to D.

Point A is in the middle between the dart and side-seam, and is the pivot from which to sweep the length from D forward to the back dart.

Forward from the back dart it runs straight across.

This forepart can be cut with only one dart, as shown on Diagrams 12 and 22, or if a loose front is preferable the darts are left out, only that the side-seam at B is reduced from 1 to 1½ inch, and a small amount is taken off at D.

Should it be desirable to have fullness or plaits only in the back, then it obviously needs no addition on the sidebody (Diagram 18) at G, but will retain the shape F of the dotted line, and of course have nothing added from D to E.

The addition of 1 inch as given will cast considerable fullness in the skirt, and for current styles is just right for jackets whose length is from 33 to 38 inches.

If, however, the coat is made 40 to 50 inches long, the spread caused by the lines drawn through the 1 inch increase would be altogether too large at bottom.

Therefore for long garments the distance to be added at D and E, or on the other points on the hip line, should be no more than ½ inch, which would give ample fullness for a long garment.

The addition to be added for a double-breasted shape may be 3 to 4 inches, and this should run parallel with the original front edge, which is represented by the dotted line.

The shape of the turnover lapel being a matter of taste, no set rule can be established.

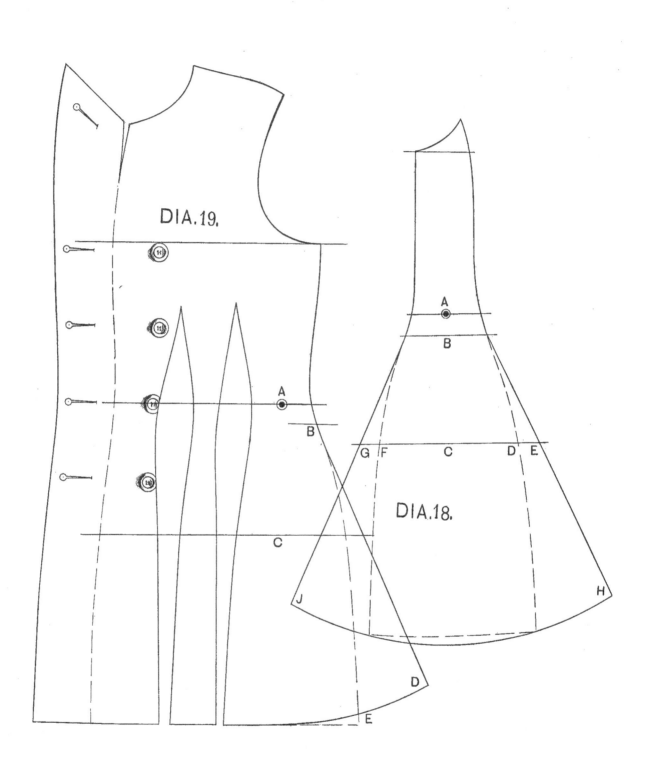

DIA. 19.

DIA. 18.

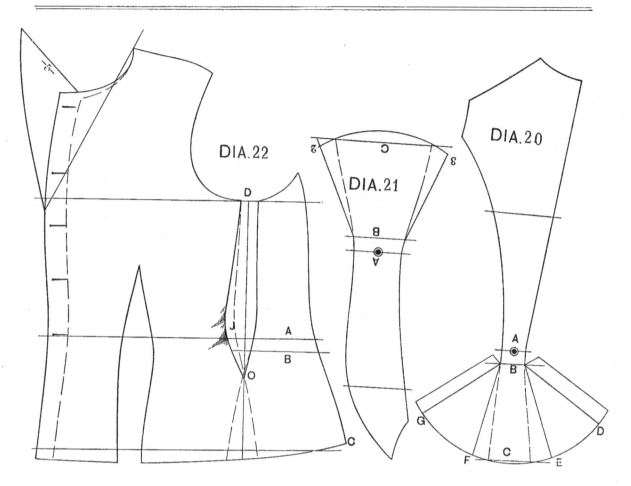

SHORT JACKET WITH PLAITED SKIRT.

DIAGRAM 20.—This pattern retains its shape above the waist as cut.

Below, any amount may be added, according to the effect desired.

By adding 4 to 6 inches on either side of the original, we gain the lines D and G, giving sufficient fullness to produce three plaits in the back skirt. That from E to D being the one in the center, and F to G those on the sides. From A, as pivot, sweep the length each way from C.

DIAGRAM 21.—For a short jacket the sidebody should not have too much fullness, and therefore an addition of from 1 to 1½ inch at 1 and 2 will be about right.

DIAGRAM 22.—This is plain, with only one dart, with a reduction in size on the side-seam. It is usually cut with the sidebody attached from O downward.

In such cases overlap the sidebody and front below the hip till the distance between them is 1 inch at D.

The dart is then only cut as far down as O, and a little more spring added at C.

The amount added for lap at front is 1 inch, and two styles of turnover for the lapel are shown.

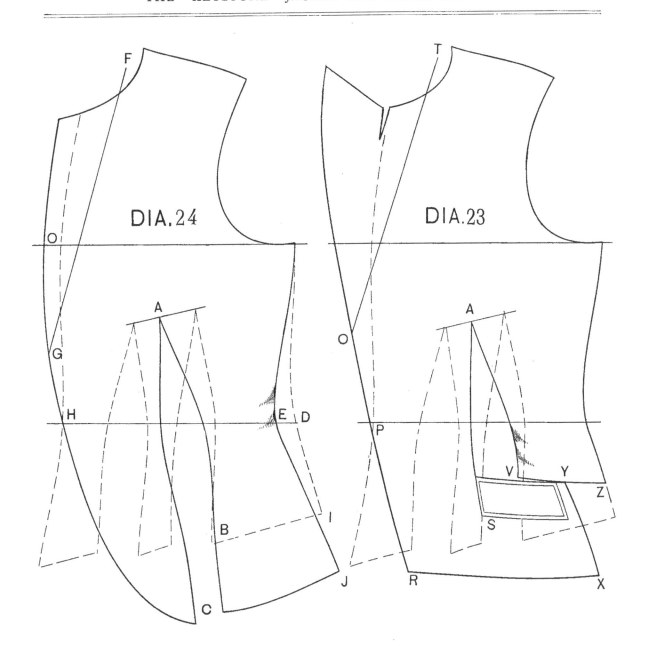

CUTAWAY JACKETS.

DIAGRAM 23.—This diagram shows what deviation can be made from the original draft, as shown by the dotted lines, when two darts are drawn in.

First it is decided to have the front edge to run from O past P back to R.

The front dart, as usually cut, would reach R just at the corner, resulting in rather a bad effect. To prevent this we transfer the dart to the middle between the two and draw it backward at the bottom, so that its front-seam will be very nearly parallel with that of the front edge.

We locate the pocket and let the dart reach only to its front end.

The width of the dart, which can be made as large as both darts for a close fit, may, however, be only ⅔ of both darts, the ⅓ left over being no detriment to a cutaway jacket—in fact, rather beneficial.

As point V will be sewn to the front of the pocket, so will point Z reach to Y, and therefore the side-seam will run from Y to X, less the amount of the width of the dart.

DIAGRAM 24.—This shows a cutaway, with 1 inch added over the center line at O and G, and cut away just on the front edge at H.

If we extend the two darts down to the bottom, the first one will cut directly in the curve of the front.

In order to obviate the bad effect this would produce, we cut out only one dart and start it backward beyond the curve, or in such a position that below the waist line it will very nearly run parallel with the side-seam.

This one dart may be the full size of the two required, or only the size of one; but in the latter case reduce on the side-seam, from D to E, ½ of a dart as shown

---

COVERT JACKET.

DIAGRAM 25.—Use the regular block pattern of the size needed; lay it down on a sheet of paper, and mark along the shoulder, top of the back and back-seam, and extend the length as far down as required, as to F.

Then place the sidebody against the back, touching at points O and B, in the same closing position to the back as when drafted.

Follow the pattern along the side-seam, C to D, passing E and continuing to K.

DIAGRAM 26.—The front is produced by the block pattern, and marked along the edges, armhole, shoulder, neck and front.

One to one-and-a-half inch below the waist line lay the sidebody against the front, touching at point A in such a position that its upper part will be 1 inch away from the front at the armhole.

In this position it overlaps at the bottom, B.

Now shape from C to D, and regulate the length to D by the length of the back.

Sweep the curve at bottom from the shoulder point, flattening it toward the front.

For a single-breasted front add to the front edge 1 inch; for a fly front 1½ inch, and for a double-breasted front 2½ to 3 inches. Form the lapel to any desired shape.

The cut under the arm reaches only to A.

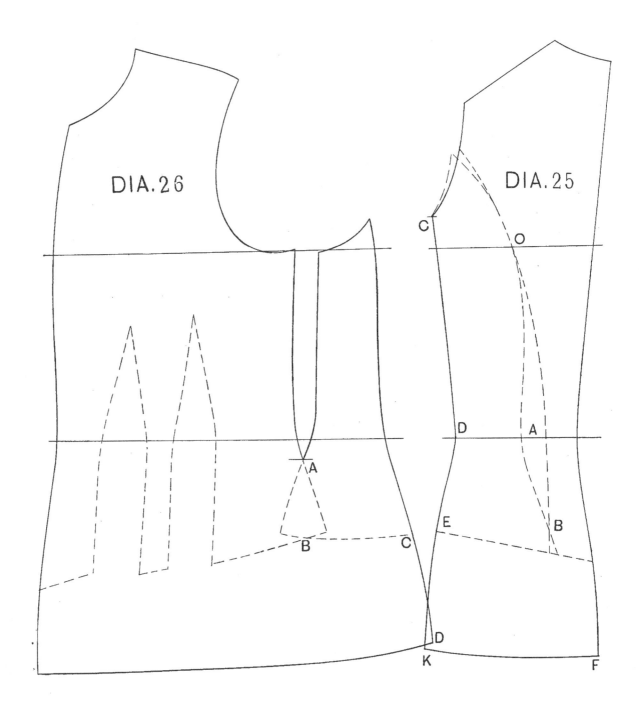

DIA. 26

DIA. 25

FROCK COAT.

DIAGRAM 27.—This pattern is drafted the same as explained for Diagram 7, 8 or 9, with the following exceptions:

Below the waist line add 1 to 1½ inch; form the lower edges of the body, and draw in the skirt as for a sack jacket, either wide or narrow at bottom. Establish the length to C and add 1 inch for plait on the side and the same on the center of back at E and C.

DIAGRAM 28.—A straight line is drawn as A to C, and the forepart is laid against it, touching at the fullest part of the breast and at the waist B.

Go upward from B ½ of the waist measure, which gives the black dot.

From the dot, as pivot, sweep from B over, giving the upper-seam of the skirt (Diagram 29) to F.

Mark off the size from B to 1, which is to the first dart. Then place the piece between the darts, K, against 1, which will reach to 2. Then the width from O to S is placed from 2, fixing 3. Next, the first sidebody, M, is laid from 3 and reaches to 4.

Now we take the other sidebody and lay its lower seam from 4 along the curve, and this will reach to F.

Holding the sidebody in this position, draw a straight line from its upper point at G through F, which will bring it through and below H.

The next thing is to take the length of the back skirt and place it from B to C. By the dot at A, as pivot, we sweep the bottom of the skirt from C back to the line F H.

This line is not fully extended, on account of lack of width on the plate.

DIAGRAM 30: THE LAPEL.—Mark along the edge of front of the forepart and across the bottom, V to W.

Establish the length, V to U, the same as forepart. Make the width at bottom ½ inch less than from the front edge to the edge of the first dart.

Make it 3½ inches wide across the breast, and at the top any width desired.

Lay the lapel in a closing position to B and breast (Diagram 28), and mark down the front edge of the skirt from D to E.

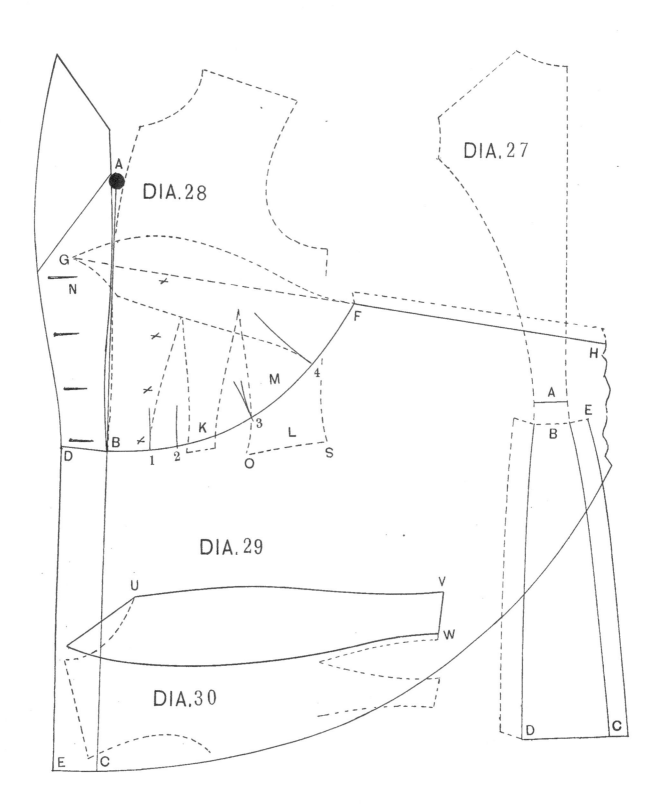

CUTAWAY FROCK JACKET.

DIAGRAMS 31 AND 32.

THE body is drafted to measure in the regular way.

The back is extended down to the length needed, and the amount for the side plait and the turn-in added.

To make the skirt we first lay down the sidebody and draw along its lower edge from G to H, as shown on Diagram 32.

Lay a long rule stick at the top of the sidebody, point D, and touching the waist line at E, and draw a line along the edge from G to F.

Apply the length of the back skirt from G to obtain point F, and then draw a short right-angled line at the bottom.

Lay the second sidebody (E) against H. This will reach to J.

In laying these pieces to get the width, they should be so closely connected that the spring below the natural waist line will be in the position as sewn up.

This must be carefully attended to, as it influences the curve of the seam of the skirt.

Next we place part O of the front from J to K also in a closing position.

Having marked K, lay the middle piece between the darts to K. This will go to N, and when the front Q is added will reach to L.

The line now will be G to H, J to K, and K to L. Curve the line of the skirt from K to M ¾ inch below L.

Now place the forepart in a closing position, L to M, and draw the curve of the skirt from M through W and X, to the shape most desirable.

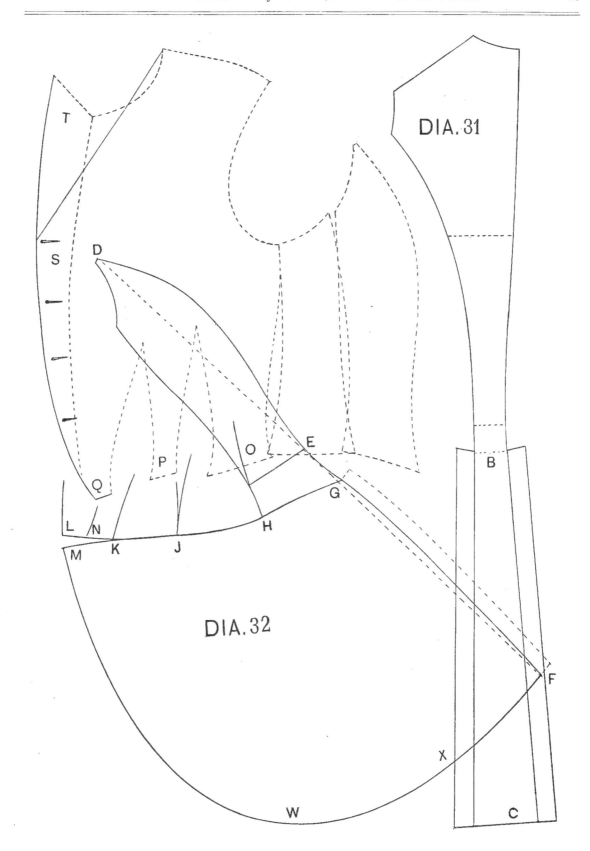

DIA. 31

DIA. 32

DOUBLE-BREASTED RIDING JACKET.

DIAGRAM 33.

THIS is drafted like a sack jacket and extends down in the back and on the side length to 28 inches.

The darts are placed in the position they should occupy; the length in front is made 3 to 3½ inches longer than the natural waist, and the skirt is cut off from G at the last dart.

It is not necessary to enlarge the width of skirt; it should be made up just to the size of the hip.

The fronts are double-breasted as shown, and require a narrow turndown collar.

All the lines and points are closely cut to the system.

The lapel is cut on the same lines as those shown on Diagram 30.

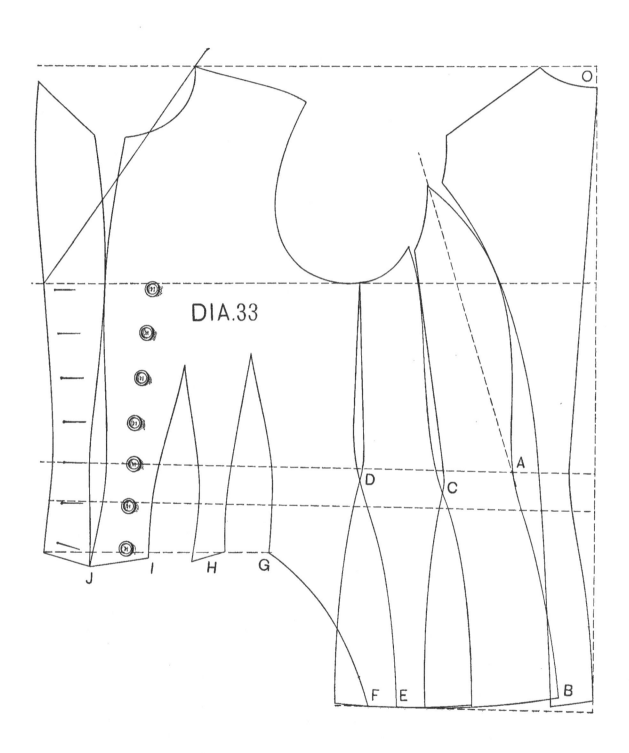

DIA.33

SINGLE-BREASTED RIDING JACKET.

DIAGRAM 34.—This style is drafted the same as a waist pattern with the waist extended below the natural waist line from 1 to 2 inches, and either shaped as shown or made more pointed in front.

The skirt is cut separate and reaches only to the second dart, the front seam of which is lengthened to agree with the width of the strap of the skirt; the front being also lengthened as represented by the broken lines.

This draft has three sidebodies, as it is desirable that the width between the seams should be narrow in order to better define the form. These sidebodies should each have about the same width at the waist line.

For a single-breasted front, add for lap on the button-hole side no more than ¾ inch, and about as much more for the button stand   If 3 or more hooks and eyes are sewn to the center line inside it will relieve the strain on the buttons.

It can be made to button up with a standing collar, or with a short roll and turnover collar.

THE SKIRT.

DIAGRAM 35.—Draw a straight line as O B.

From O down to A is ¼ of the waist, which for a 24 waist is 6 inches.

From O as pivot, sweep a circle from A toward H.

Take the sidebody and lay it with its lower point at A, and so that the waist line will rest on the line at 4.

In this position the lower edge will not rest on the sweep, but rise above it at 1.

Now draw along it from A to 1.

Take the next sidebody, close it to 1, and let the forward point rest on the sweep point 2.

Draw a line at a right angle from O to E, and from D the point on the circle to E will be 1 inch.

Now from 2 through E draw the curve to F.

From 2 to 3 lay the third sidebody to obtain the width, and then place the part of the front from K to S from 3, reaching to F.

F to the outside edge, Z, is 1½ inch.

From 2 to Y is the same.

The bottom, B to C, is 2½ inches, and is shaped past X to C like the diagram.

A side plait is added to A and B of the same width as that on the back.

After all is drawn out, the upper seam of the skirt is the line from A to 1, 2, 3 and F.

DIAGRAM 36.—The back is regular down to the waist, where it is usually made very narrow—about 1 inch on line A. The skirt, which is then added to C, is never more than 8 nor less than 6 inches long from B to C.

NOTE.—The sleeve head for these garments is never so large as for other jackets, but is held small or with only a small rise to cause a puff, and the wrist is made small to close with buttons. When a sleeve is made to close at the wrist, it necessitates buttons, and for the prevailing style it is necessary to make the upper sleeve narrower at wrist, so that the buttons shall be on top of the wrist, as shown on Diagram 44.

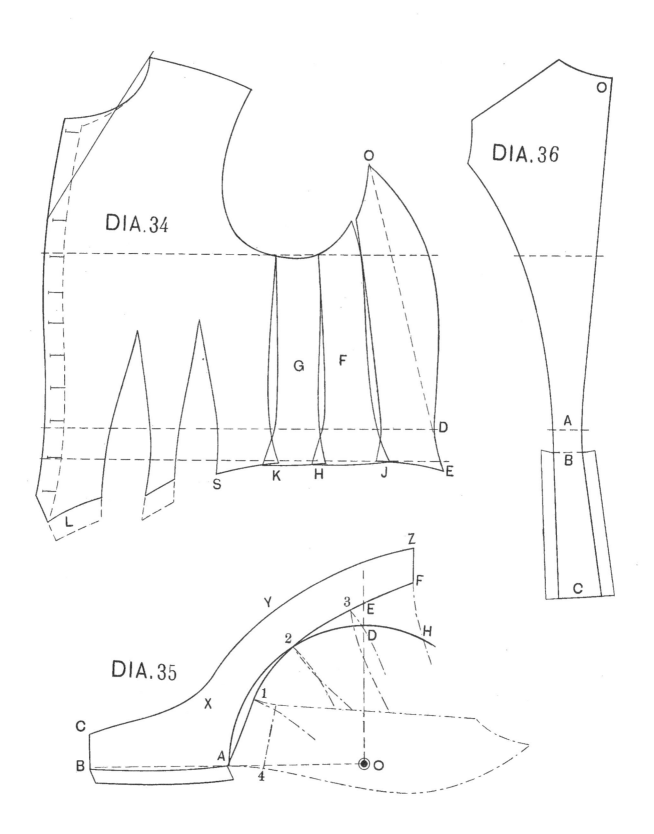

SHIRT WAISTS.

THE FOREPART.

DIAGRAM 37.—First use a waist pattern either to measure or proportions.

Draw a straight line from O to R, and lay the pattern down against it at breast and waist, as represented by the broken lines.

Mark along the arm-hole and lay the first sidebody in a closing position to the front at arm-hole and overlaping just 1 inch below the waist.

Draw a line along its side to W.

Now place in front of O and R 6 to 10 inches, according to the amount of fullness desired to be gathered in, as to P and S.

Curve the line on top of shoulder ½ inch above it, and draw the line P S.

The distance P V must be gathered in to that of O V, and when finished the pattern is laid against the armhole and the neck cut by it.

A yoke of lining can also be cut of the shape at the shoulder and neck, and the material gathered on to it.

THE BACK.

DIAGRAM 38.—On a straight line like O E lay the back center-seam.

Then place the sidebody close to the back at the top and 1½ inch from it at the waist, as shown.

Now mark along the armhole from K to G, and along the side from G to L and N.

Even with the top of back draw a line to C.

From O to C place the same amount added to the front from O to P, and draw a straight line to F.

Apply the length, which is generally 21 inches, from O to E and shape the bottom.

Raise above shoulder at B ½ inch.

When the length has been fixed at N, apply the length from G to N to the front, to finish the bottom.

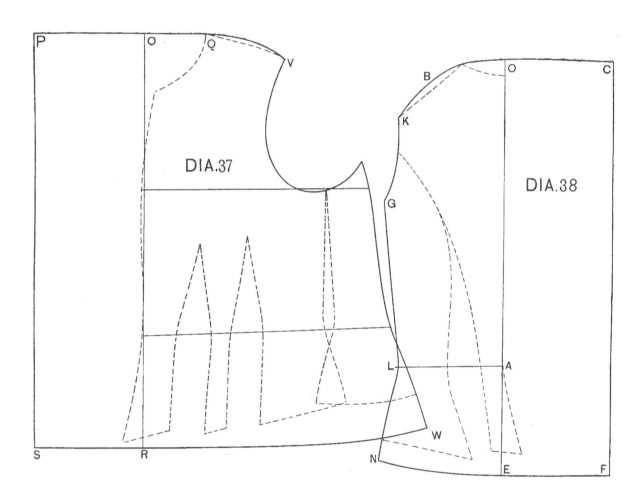

SHIRT WAIST WITH YOKE.

THE BACK.

DIAGRAM 39.—Take the waist and mark along the armhole from T, along the shoulder top of the back, and down the back to B more or less low, as may be desired.

This will be the yoke pattern, and must be cut out of another sheet of paper.

Then draw a line along the back-seam from O to E and D.

Lay the sidebody close to the back at T and within 1½ inch of it at K.

Mark around it from T to J, J to H and G, and apply the length from O to D for the bottom.

Square lines from B to C and from D to F.

Place 6 to 8 inches from B to C and D to F, and draw the line C F.

From C curve above B 2 inches to T.

THE FOREPART.

DIAGRAM 40.—Lay the forepart against a straight line, as R N.

Point S is opposite point T on the back, when J is laid close to the top of the sidebody.

From S to P curve the line for the yoke, which will be the shape of the shoulder and this line.

The sidebody is laid close against the front at the armhole and overlaps 1 inch below the waist line. Mark along the side-seam to L and M.

Apply the length of the back to the front, and curve from M forward.

From P to Q place the same amount as on the back, and the same from N to O ; now draw the straight line O Q.

From S to Q curve the upper part 2 inches above P to R.

The material between S and Q is gathered into the distance P S, and that of the back into T B.

A band is usually sewn inside the waist, to which the waist amount is gathered, but sometimes the waist is left loose and worn inside of a skirt, the back of which holds it close.

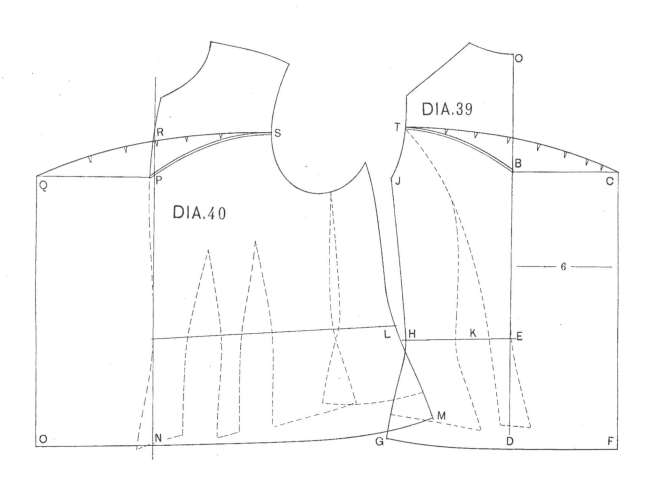

THE PLAIN SLEEVE.

WHEN the waist, basque or jacket is drafted, measure the armhole all around, being careful to obtain the actual circumference.

By the size obtained we draft the sleeve head.

We then require the length to the wrist, the elbow and wrist size.

As an example, we shall use the following measures :

Armhole,	-	-	-	-	-	-	16.
Length of sleeve under arm,			-	-	-		16½.
Width at elbow,		-	-	-	-	-	12.
Width at wrist,	-	-	-	-	-	-	10.

DIAGRAM 41.—Commence by drawing lines O C and O J at right angles.

O to A is ⅓ armhole, 5⅜ inches.

O to J is ½ armhole, 8 inches.

Draw a line down from J to F, and across from A to G.

From A to C is the length, 16½ inches.

B is in the middle between A and C.

C over to D is ½ wrist size and ½ inch.

From D to E is 1¾ inch.

Connect E with F by a straight line.

Point H is in the middle between O and J.

Point I is in the middle between J and H.

DIAGRAM 42.—G up to K is ¼ armhole, 4 inches.

Now, with a pair of compasses, sweep from K by H toward P, and from H by K. This gives point P, where both sweeps cross.

Now use P as pivot and sweep from K to S. This curve will touch the upper line at H and give a suitable round for the sleeve head.

Raise above A to R ½ inch, and with a slight curve connect with the sweep as shown.

Draw a short line from K to line I, which gives N, and make L 2 inches from A.

Shape the under-arm scye from R to the line at L and up to N, curving above and below a straight line from N to L, as represented.

From F forward to M is ½ of elbow width.

Draw straight lines M to A and C, and curve inside of these as shown.

DIAGRAM 43.—Work out the outlines as follows :

Shape from K to G, past F, clearing it by ¼ inch, and thence with an easy curve to E at bottom. Curve the edge of cuff from C to E.

Point 9 is ½ inch back from E, and should be straight across from E. Curve from C to 9.

Draw the elbow-seam of the under part from N to 1 straight down, and thence to Q and 9, making Q ½ inch inside of the straight line at F.

The inside-seam of the under side follows that of the upper sleeve from A through T to C.

This finishes the plain sleeve.

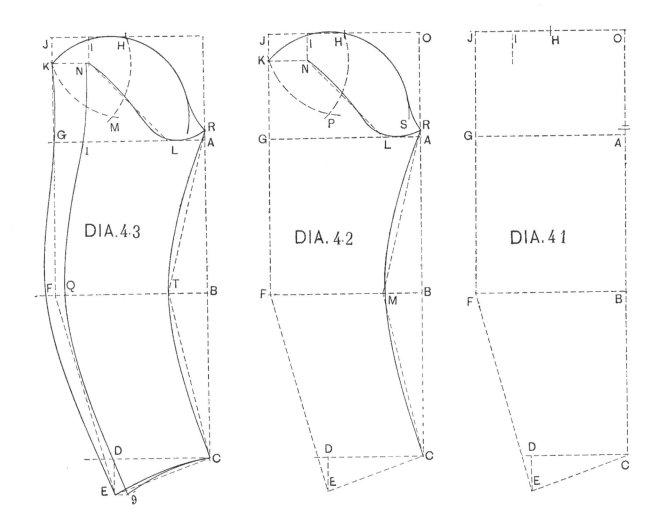

DIA. 4·3

DIA. 4·2

DIA. 4·1

CHANGES FROM THE PLAIN SLEEVE.

DIAGRAM 44.—When the shoulders are drafted narrower than given by the system proper, it is necessary to add to the sleeve top the amount the width of the shoulder has been reduced; this amount, which may be ½ to 1 inch, must be added above 2 to 3, and the curve drawn as shown from 1 through 3 to 4.

The under sleeve requires no change.

It is sometimes desirable, when a vent with buttons is required, as on close wrists for riding jackets or dresses, to reduce the width of top at wrist 1 inch, with the intention of having the button show more forward on the hand.

With the view of effecting this, go in from P on the upper sleeve 1 inch to S, and draw the elbow-seam from 6 to S.

Then draw the under sleeve from 5 at elbow to P, and add a stand for the buttons.

DIAGRAM 45.—It is often desirable to change the seams in order that they shall lie more under the arm, or sew into the sidebody instead of the back.

To accomplish this, draw a line across on the ordinary sleeve, R to X, and fix a point in the middle Q.

Point A, the dot, is point F on Diagram 41.

Go down from Q to O ¾ or 1 inch, and sweep from O over toward S and Y, pivoting at A.

Continue the sleeve head curve from R to Y, and from where it crosses the sweep at Y redraw the back-seam to the elbow near A.

As the width of the upper sleeve has been increased, we take the distance R Y and reduce the seam from X to S that amount, and from this point draw the under sleeve to the elbow.

From the front line at 9 fix a point 1 inch on the under sleeve at V. Now, pivoting at T, sweep from 9 to V U, which makes the length from T to U the same as from T to V.

Now draw the inside-seams from V to T and U to the same place, U being also 1 inch from 9. Then curve from P to U.

DIAGRAM 46.—This is made the same as the last one, only there is more space between 6 and 5.

Establish A, 1½ to 2 inches below F, and make the sweep by O at elbow.

Remodel the sleeve head from E to 5 by extending the curve of the upper part, and from where it crosses the sweep draw the elbow-seam

Take off what has been added—E to 5—from the under sleeve—D to 4—and from 4 draw to 2.

The same amount may be taken off on the inside as on Diagram 45, if so desired, or it may be left as shown, without any change.

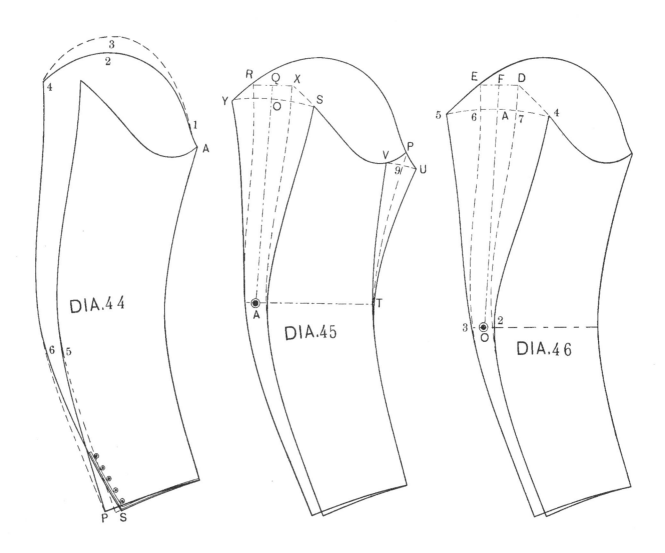

LARGE SLEEVE HEAD.

DIAGRAM 47.

TAKE a regularly cut sleeve, and on this mark a line through the center, O A, and also mark the elbow line.

Lay it down on a sheet of paper and mark along it from the elbow down, H to 10 and G to T, and across from T to 10.

The upper part is shown by P and S.

From S by H sweep to F.

From P by G sweep to R.

Draw a line straight across the top of sleeve head—each way from A—at right angles with line O A.

A to C is 2½ inches, and C to D is the same.

Go over from A to N 3 inches, and the same from A to B, and square up from these points.

Hold the sleeve at H and swing it over at top till point A will rest on line B 7, and when in this position draw along its edge from F to H and F to 9.

Shape the top from 9 upward in a nearly straight line to E, and from thence through 8 to D as represented.

Points 8 and E are not established, except by the run of this curve, which must be directed by the eye.

Put the pattern in the first position, and holding it at G move it over till A rests on line N ; then mark the elbow line, R to G.

To obtain the back curve we place the distance from the line at 7 to 8 over from 6 to fix 5, and that of B to E over from N to get 3. Through these points shape the sleeve head.

This large sleeve is shown by the solid black lines R, D, E and F, H 10 and R, G and T.

The under sleeve is not changed.

This gives a good, fairly full sleeve; but if one is wanted quite full, take the one just made, lay it down on paper, and proceed as follows :

Place the under sleeve against the upper at the wrist, T, and closing about 2 inches below the elbow, as shown on the diagram.

It will overlap a trifle at M, but this is of no consequence. The object is to keep the elbow width nearly the same and not change the wrist in size.

In this position we gain all the distance between R and 2, which is the amount it increases in size.

Now draw along the front-seam F to 10, up from F to D, and from D curve past 4 to 2 in such a shape that the line will have a curve between 4 and D similar to that between D and 9.

This sleeve has no back-seam, as its outer edge is the one shown on the diagram Z, 2, D, F, 10 and G.

In sewing it into the armhole it requires a heavy box-plait on the center of top at Y and a series of side plaits on each side of this point until it has been reduced to the size of the armhole.

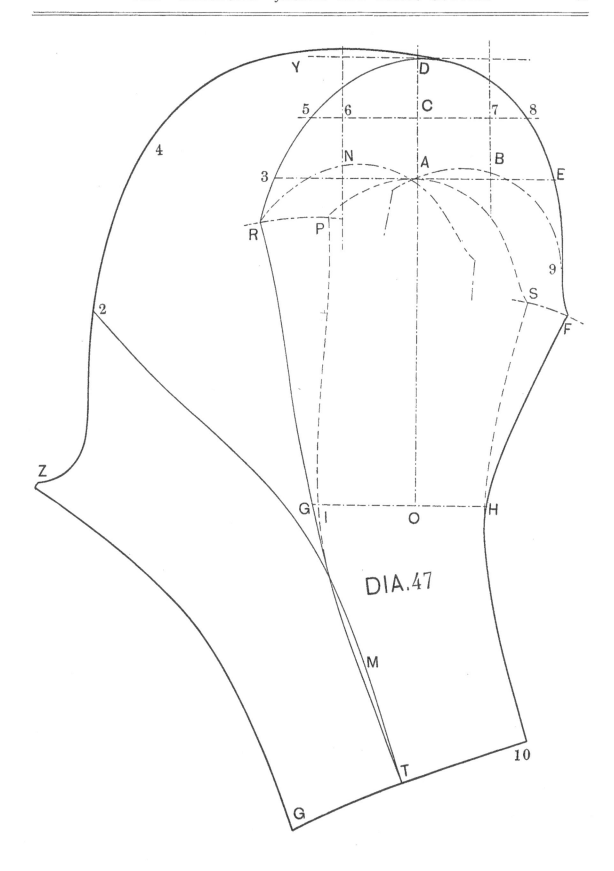

DIA. 47

A VERY FULL SLEEVE.

DIAGRAM 48.

THIS sleeve can be easily held as close from the elbow down as an ordinary sleeve, as follows :

Take any sleeve pattern—upper and lower parts—and draw a straight center line from F to G, to which mark line Y X at right angles.

Lay the upper and the under sleeve with the elbow at H, so that they will be separated at G 1½ inch. *This is correct when the wrist of the sleeve used is small, but when of medium size the distance should be only 1 inch.*

Mark along the edges of the patterns used from X and Y down.

Using X as pivot sweep over from point R, which will go to 2.

According to the size wanted, or the volume of fullness in the upper part, we add on the sweep from R to 2 either 3 inches for medium or 4 for an extra large sleeve. Then holding the pattern used at X, swing it over until point R reaches 2, and then follow along its inside edge from 2 to X for the seam.

By Y on the lower sleeve sweep from O toward point 3 from Q.

Now add from Q to 3 on the sweep the same amount as has been added on the upper sleeve from R to 2, which gives point 3 ; and pivoting at Y, swing the inside sleeve forward to 3, and shape the in-seam from 3 to Y.

Draw a straight line from 2 to 3 ; this gives us point P.

P to O is 4 inches. Making O the pivot, sweep the upper curve from 6, passing F and 4 and reaching 5.

As we must retain some semblance of an under-arm, we reduce this sweep from 4 to 3 by going inside of 5 about 1½ inch.

This sleeve closes with buttons and has a strip 1¼ inch wide sewed on the under sleeve to act as a button stand.

It may sometimes be advisable to have the buttons run toward the top of wrist. In such a case, whatever is placed forward is added to the under part, as shown.

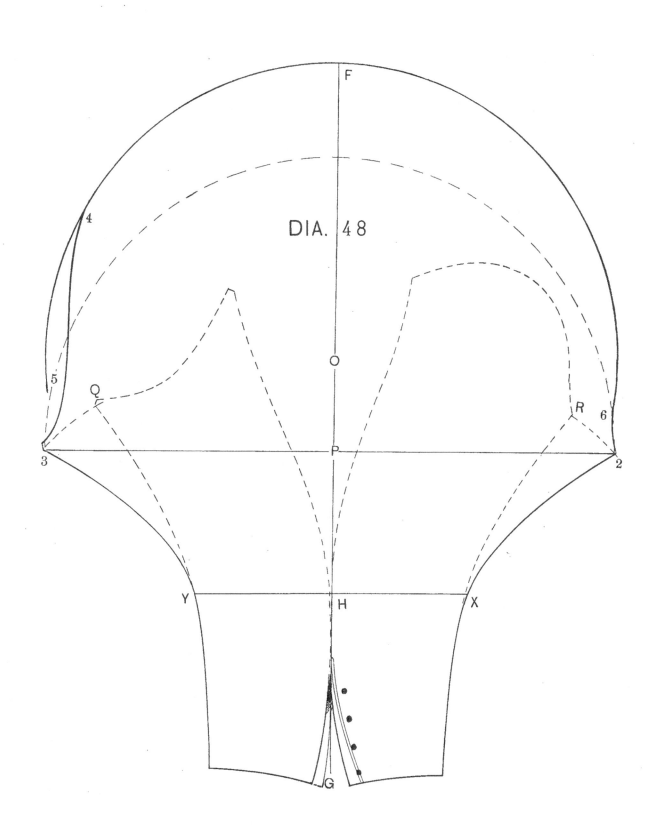

SLEEVE FOR SHIRT WAISTS.

DIAGRAM 49.—This style of sleeve is worn with shirt waists, dresses and wash fabrics.

Sometimes the sleeve head is plain or with only a slight fullness, but it may have a large and full sleeve head.

In case it is to be plain or to have only a slight fullness, use an ordinary sleeve pattern and lay the top and undersides together at the elbow O, and closing at top P, or separated only 2 or 3 inches for some little fullness.

In this position it is open at the bottom, V to Z.

The lower curve is drawn from T through Z and V to U, as illustrated.

There is no elbow-seam, as the sleeve is cut in one piece.

A modification of this sleeve is to gather it in from 1 to 2, close to the arm, which gives a loose sleeve above these points and a ruffle effect at the bottom.

This sleeve can be cut for a puff effect by using the top of a large sleeve such as has been shown.

DRESS SLEEVES.

DIAGRAMS 50 AND 51.—On low neck dress waists these sleeves are generally made short. Some reach only a few inches below the armhole and some to the elbow.

The manner of cutting is very simple.

Take a sleeve pattern and lay the upper against the lower part on the back-seams, as shown on these diagrams, and draw along the top and on the side.

Fix whatever length is wanted and cut across from W to X (Diagram 50), curving somewhat above a straight line at Y.

Another style is to curve, as shown by Diagram 51, from B to C and A.

Yet another style is, curve from C up to the middle of sleeve at U, and from U to A. This style is, however, made a little wider at U, so as to allow these two points to overlap about 1 inch.

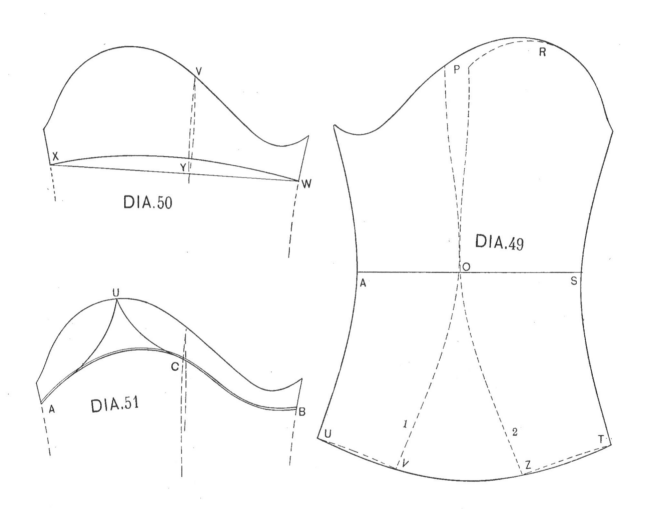

DIA.50

DIA.51

DIA.49

SINGLE-BREASTED VESTS.

DIAGRAM 52.

THE measures by which the diagram on the opposite page were produced are as follows:

Back length,	15.
Front length,	18¼.
Blade,	10.
Height under arm,	7½.
Breast,	36.
Waist,	25.
Length of front,	23.

The method of delineating is the same as for a waist pattern in the main points.

Square the lines O C and O F.   O to 1 is ¾ inch.   Measure from 1 to B, the back length 15.   B to A is the height under arm, 7½.   From both points draw lines across.

B to D is $\frac{1}{12}$ breast.   Draw the back line from 1 through D.   From this line (point A 1) to K is the blade measure, 10 inches.

This is ⅔ of a 30 size, as shown by the number 15 on the square.

Take ¼ of this, which is 3¾, and place it from K to L.

Draw a line up and down from K and one up from L.

Divide the distance L to top line in halves, which locates the star.

Point Y is in the middle between the star and the top line.   O to 2 is ⅛ of 15.

From 2 to Z, which is in the middle between the star and Y, draw a line.

Curve the armhole from X to 12.

A1 to G is one-half of the full breast, 18 inches.

In the middle between G and K locate point P, from which point a line is drawn up to E.   E to F is ⅙ breast, 3 inches.

From F through G draw a straight front line.   F to N is ⅙ breast, 3 inches.

Apply the front length from 1 inch in front of J at waist up to line E, less the width of top of back, and locate E by the measure, whether it goes above or below the top line.   In this case it falls on the top line.

From E to Y draw a line and place the distance 2 X of the back from E to locate 13, and finish the armhole.   Line K to oo is the same distance as from Z to X.

Divide the distance G K into three parts, giving points S and T.   From S go back ½ inch to U.   Also divide the distance from the front waist line at H to the side at J into 3 parts, to locate the points Q and R.

Now from U through Q draw a straight line, and draw another from T through R.   Measure the distance on the waist line from D to H, which will be found to be 18 inches.   Deduct 1 inch from this, leaving 17.

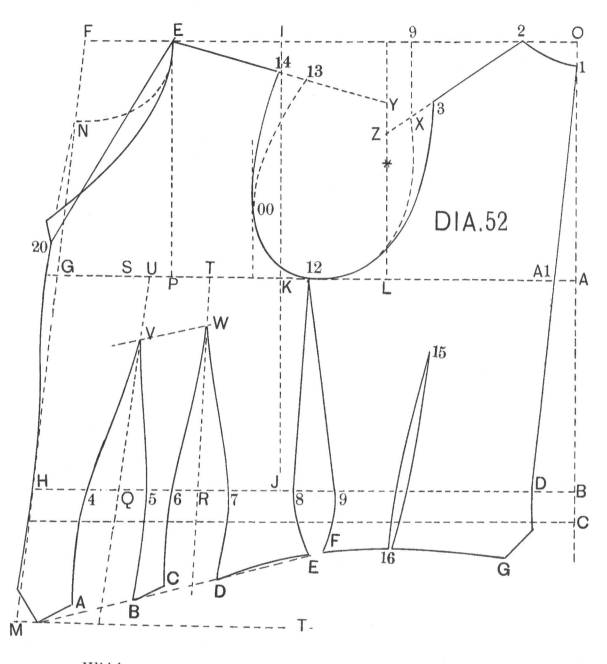

DIA. 52

Width,	-	-	-	-	-	-	17.
½ waist,	-	-	-	-	-	-	12½.
Difference,	-	-		-	-	-	4½.

This difference is to govern the darts, each of which will therefore require a width of 2⅛ inches.

Place this 2⅛ inches equally on each side of Q to 4 and 5, and of R to 6 and 7.

From the point V, which is about ⅓ way from U to Q, draw the dart lines through 4 and 5, and let the line below 4 to A be straight down, and that from 5 to B have only a slight spring from a straight line.

Draw in the seams from W through 6 and 7, holding the line from 6 to C straight, and giving that from 7 to D a little spring—say about 1 inch forward from a line drawn down at right angles with the waist line.

Divide the distance between A1 on the back and G, which gives point 12.

From D at back of waist place ½ of the waist measure and 1 inch to point 9.

From the front at H to 4, 5, 6 and 7 to 8 place ¼ of the waist less 1 inch.

Then draw in the under-arm seams from 12 through 8 and 9, adding a little spring below the waist line to E and F.

Apply the length from E to M at the bottom, which for this draft is 23 inches.

From M draw a straight line parallel with the waist line to T.

In the middle between T and 8 mark a point, which is E, and from E to M draw a straight line.

Follow this line from E to D, and a trifle above it locate C; draw to B, and then even across from B will be A. From this point draw down to the line M.

Reduce the width of shoulder from X to 3, 1 to 1½ inch, for small sizes 1 inch, but for larger sizes 1½ inch is preferable. The same must be reduced on the front shoulder from 13 to 14. The form from E to N is for a front to button up to the neck, and usually has a standing collar.

If, however, it is desired to have an open front, measure from E down the front line to point 20, the opening wanted, which may be 10, 12 or 14 inches, always remembering that the width of the top of the back must be subtracted.

Beyond G go out ½ inch, and then curve the front edge as shown.

Even with point E at the lower part of the vest draw a line across, which gives the bottom of the back—the line F to G.

As the vest is generally worn over a corset, it would be too large around the waist if cut by the measure taken over a dress, so we must reduce the size at the waist by inserting a V from 16 to 15, which will be ½ inch in width.

Diagram 53.—After following the explanations given for Diagram 52, we place above point E to 1 the width of the top of the back, which is 2 to O on the preceding diagram.

Having located the point to which we want the opening to extend—at G for instance—draw a straight line from G to the shoulder point E.

From just in front of the line squared up from E, start to curve the outer edge, drawing it so that it will be a trifle inside of the line at 4 and ending at G.

Go back from E ½ inch, make the distance 1 to 2 the same as 3 and E, and draw out the shape of the collar as shown. The collar can then be traced out on a separate piece of paper.

All the points on this diagram are drawn in the same way as those on the foregoing, but for this vest we reduce the front by one dart only.

In drafting, however, it is best to first draw both darts. Then knowing the amount which must be taken out, we can so modify it that it will be right with one dart.

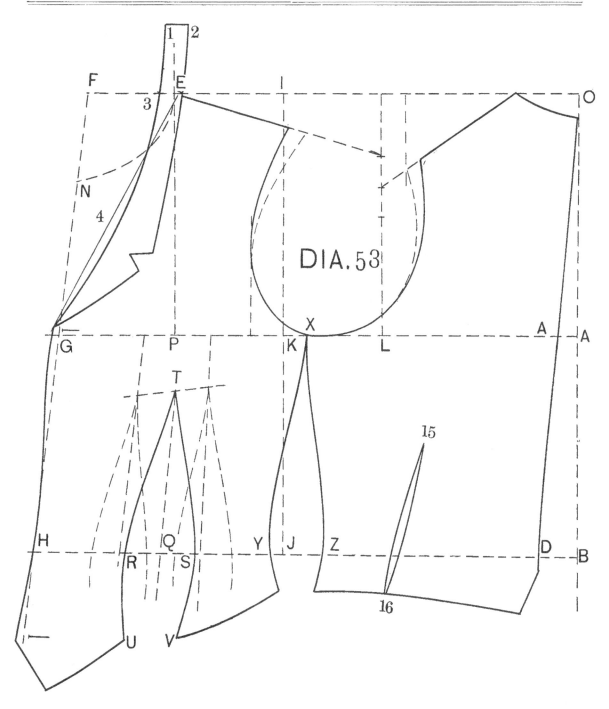

While we cannot cut out the total amount of the two darts in one, we can reduce the size by one dart by making its width from R to S ⅓ less than the full amount of the two darts, and we can then reduce to the size required under the arm at Y.

The position of the dart in the middle between the two original darts has already been so clearly explained and illustrated that it is not necessary to go over it again.

DOUBLE-BREASTED VESTS.

DIAGRAM 54.—When the draft has been drawn to the front edge, as shown on Diagram 52, add over the front edge for a double-breasted at B 1¾ to 2 inches, and at A 2½ to 3 inches, depending on the amount of lap-over you wish.

As the button-holes must always be ¾ inch from the edge, it will be necessary to take the distance from the end of the button-holes to the center line, and place this back from the center of the front to locate the place for the buttons.

On Diagram 53 we have shown the manner of arranging the collar on a flat surface. In the case of double-breasted fronts the same method can be followed by drawing the break line from the shoulder point to the point of opening at A wherever this may be desired.

Add above O to 1 the width of the top of the back, and draw the break line with some curve below O, as shown by the dotted line.

Next shape the collar as shown by the dotted line, or in any other form that may suggest itself.

In drafting a collar by what may be called the old method, make the break line straight from O to A, but instead of following this as for a flat collar, we commence at O and curve the seam-edge by C and to about 1 inch above A ; we then extend from O to 2 the width of back, and draw the stand from D through C, along the curve to A, after which we shape the outer edge from 1 to A, according to taste or style.

The two darts inserted in this forepart should always be put into vests, the material of which is hard to make ; but on soft goods one dart, as shown on Diagram 55, will answer as well.

DIAGRAM 55.—On this diagram we have a change, which is generally desirable, as the seam between the forepart and the lapel gives the garment a close fit without the aid of extra work in shrinking in the edge.

In cutting the lapel, follow the same rule as that used in drafting the double-breasted jacket, Diagram 28.

Trace along the front edge of the forepart from E to B, and keep the same shape from B to J.

Make the width from B to J 1½ to 2 inches, and across at D 2½ to 3 inches, and form the edge from J to D.

Lay it over as on the diagram, touching at B and E, and draft the collar the same as shown on Diagram 54.

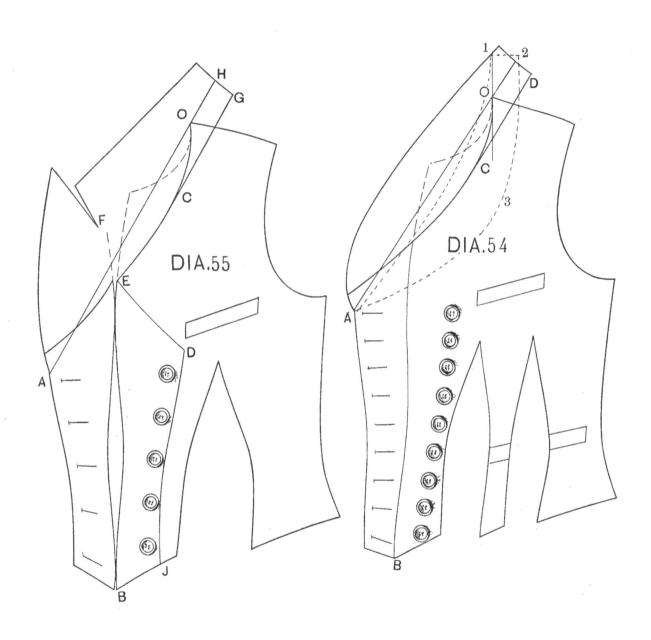

DIA. 55

DIA. 54

COLLARS.

DIAGRAM 56.—In cutting collars, the predominant idea must be to design them for the purpose for which they are intended.

The different styles illustrated on the plate on the opposite page will enable any one to draft whatever style may be desired.

Let us first draft Diagram 56. This is a collar that clings close to the neck on the upper edge, and is one that is preferred above all others for some dress waists.

To draft it we draw lines O 1 and O 4.

From O to 1 is ½ of the neck size, and from O to 4 the width we prefer, which may be 2 to 3 inches.

From 1 to 2 place the same width as O to 4 and curve the edge, which sews on the neck ½ inch below the straight line O 1, and retreat the front from 2 to 3 about ½ to ¾ inch.

DIAGRAM 57.—This collar is drawn on square lines by placing from O to 1 the size of neck, and adding whatever width is needed above O to 4.

This collar will not cling to the neck as close as that of Diagram 56.

DIAGRAM 58.—This form will not cling to the neck on the upper edge, because of the curve from 3 to 4.

In drafting it draw the lines C 2 and C 4.

From C go up to O 1 inch, and form the neck line from O to 2 as shown.

Add the width to 4 and 3 and finish as represented.

DIAGRAM 59.—With the view of giving more curve to the upper edge and therefore more flare to it, we are compelled to make the distance A to B 2½ inches.

Apply the size of the neck from A to D, the width from B to C, and finish as shown on the diagram.

DIAGRAM 60.—This collar is similar to that of Diagram 59, and it is the most useful of all collars, as it adapts itself not only to a standing form, but is equally as good to turn down for a short roll front. The manner of construction is exactly the same as explained for Diagram 59.

DIAGRAM 61.—When we desire to perfect the collar which is ordinarily termed "The Medeciè," we are compelled to raise above point A to B 3 inches.

Applying the size of neck from A to D, curving the neck-seam from B to D, and adding the width B to C and D to E will finish this style.

DIAGRAM 62.—This is the extremest plain style that it is possible to make for a collar that will stand up and that can also be turned down.

This is also called "The Medeciè," and may be curved in front as shown on this diagram, or shaped as shown on Diagram 61; that is, straight up in the front.

DIAGRAM 63.—This represents an ordinary turn-down collar for a single-breasted, three-button cutaway, sack or frock.

First decide on the distance that it may be wished to turn, say 4½ inches below the top at 7, marked on the diagram as point W.

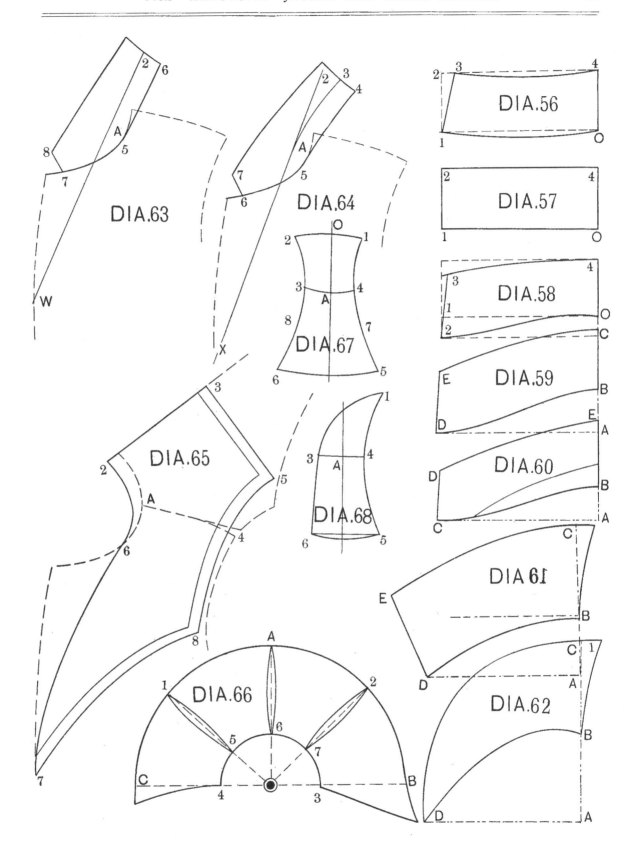

From the side at neck, 5, to the break line at point A is ¾ inch; now draw a straight line from W through A to 2.

From 2 to 6 is 1 inch, and 2 to the outside edge is 1¼ to 1½ inch.

Shape from 6 to 5 and follow the neck to the front at 7. The width, 7 to 8, is 1¾ inch.

DIAGRAM 64.—Proceed the same as just explained to A, then from A curve the break line toward 3, which is 1 inch below point 2.

The stand is then added to 4, and the balance finished as shown.

The object in thus curving the lines is to obtain a longer edge line which will turn smoother when made wide.

DIAGRAM 65.—This sailor-collar is drafted by the back and front shoulder, which are laid in a closing position.

Place point 2 about ¾ inch above the top of the back, curve the neck of the collar from 2 to 6 at the side of the neck, and then continue with a slight curve to 7, or as low as desired.

The distance from the top of back to 3 is decided by the depth wanted, and the width reaches to the armhole. It may be shaped as shown here, or as represented on Diagram 69 or 70.

DIAGRAM 66.—Shows a circular collar, which is drafted by the size of the neck.

First measure the neck of the pattern cut.

This we shall suppose to be 15 inches.

Take of this ⅓, 5 inches, and place it from 4 to 3. Mark a point in the center. By this point sweep the circle 4, 5, 6, 7 and 3.

Add from 4 to C the depth wanted, which may extend partly over the sleeve.

When the collar is wanted straight down, flat on the back, draw the center-seam on line 4 to C; but when it is wanted to flare, add 1 inch beyond C and curve the seam from 4.

The front edge can be cut from 3 to B, or as represented.

This collar, if cut in one piece, will stand straight out over the shoulder; but when it must have a flare, cut through at 6 to A, 7 to 2, and 5 to 1, and take out a trifle on each side of a straight line as shown.

If still more flare is wanted on the outer edge, then instead of cutting out, we add at 1, A and 2, overlaping 1 inch at each point, and thus increasing the length of the outer edge.

The pieces having been cut can have the collar added, and each piece will appear like Diagram 67. The lower part is the cape part proper, which goes over the shoulder; the upper added part is the standing collar, with a shape like the piece 3 to 4, 8 to 7, the curves being alike, or similar to the shape of the cape.

DIAGRAM 68.—The front piece of the cape and collar is usually curved back as from 3 to 1, but the line 4 to 1 is shaped by the line 5 to 4.

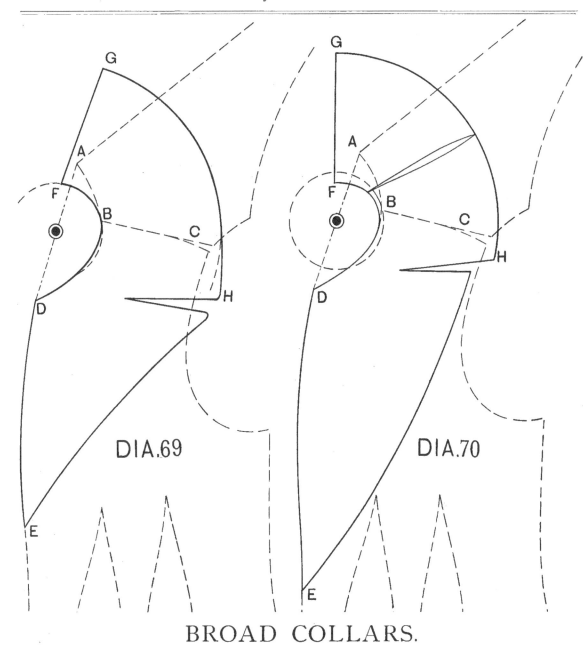

DIA. 69

DIA. 70

BROAD COLLARS.

DIAGRAM 69.—Lay the back and forepart together on the shoulder, and draw a line from top of back, A, to front, D.

Place the circled point half-way between A and D, and, pivoting at that point, draw a circle from the side of the neck, B, to reach to F.

From F draw a line parallel with line A D, as to G, making the width, F G, to fancy.

From the circled dot sweep the outer edge from G to H, form the balance by the neck and shape the lapel.

DIAGRAM 70.—This collar is very similar to the foregoing, but has more fullness cast over the shoulder. The curve is raised ½ inch above the circle at F, and the line to G is placed 2 inches further forward. The shape is then drafted by circling from G to H.

The front of the neck can be dropped at D as shown, with a view to opening it.

FULL ROUND COLLAR.

DIAGRAM 71.—Make the small circle by the diameter of the neck; draw a straight line through its center; make B to C the length required, and sweep the outer circle, pivoting at the dot.

This collar may be drawn pointed in the back to D and with two points in front at E and F, as represented.

THREE-QUARTER CAPE.

DIAGRAM 72.—Lay the back against a straight line at A and 1½ inch from it at D.

Next lay the shoulder of the front ½ inch from that of the back.

Now draw along the neck from A to B and E, and down in front E to F.

Mark a straight line from A to E, and in the middle place the dot.

Place the length wanted from A to D, and sweep the bottom by the dot as pivot.

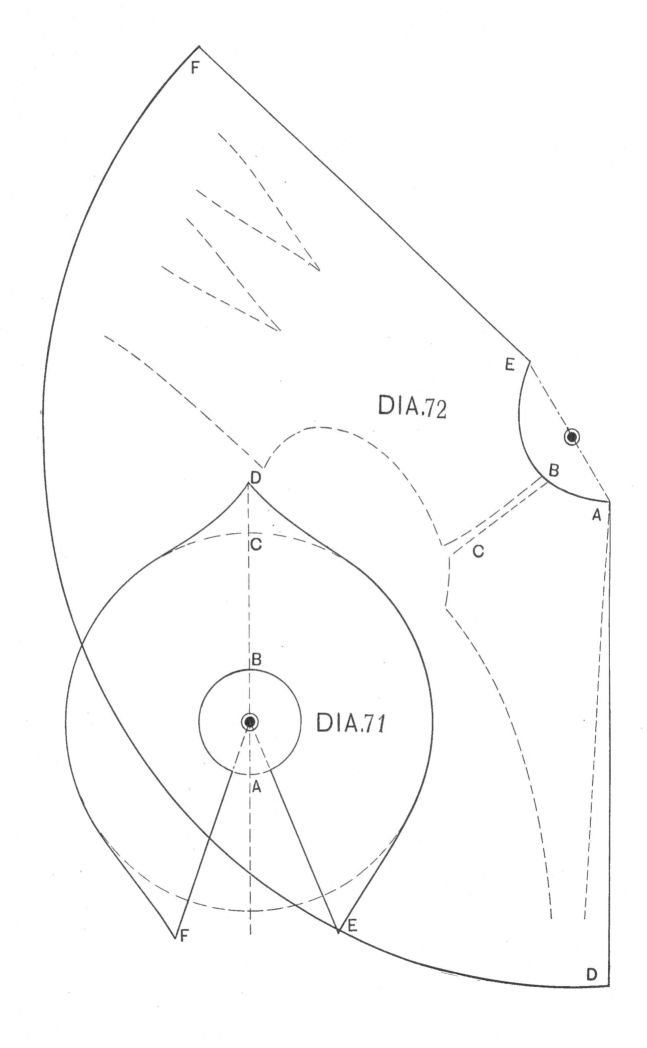

F

DIA.72

E

B

A

D

C

C

B

A

DIA.71

E

F

D

PLAIN CAPE.

DIAGRAM 73.—Lay the back against a straight line as shown, mark along the top and add to the shoulder, E to D, ½ inch. From D as pivot cast a short sweep, E to F.

Now lay the front against D, the shoulder point resting on the sweep ; open so far that the straight front edge of the forepart will be at a right angle with the back line, and then draw line G H to the dot.

Apply the length, A to C, and from the circled dot at the corner sweep the bottom.

WRAP-SHAPED CAPE.

DIAGRAM 74.—This cape is drafted in the same way on the shoulder as the plain cape, but it has a wrap shape, and, with the view of giving the back a closer fit to the figure, it is curved at B.

The bottom is curved from G, and the front reaches down 10 or 20 inches in a tab, either straight or curved back. Both styles are represented. For finish, apply lace or fur to the edge and add a high collar.

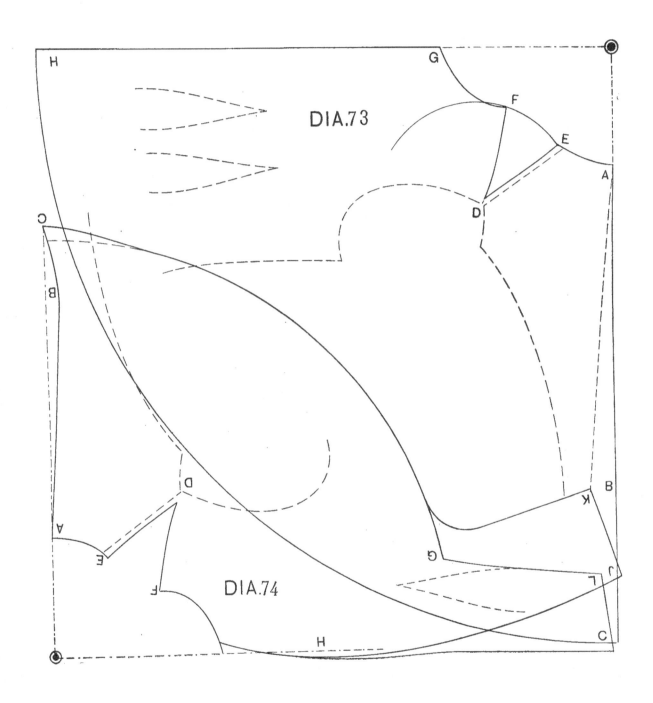

DIA.73

DIA.74

THE ULSTER.

DIAGRAM 75.—Commence to draft as for a jacket and apply the length, which goes to the floor and ranges from 52 to 56 inches.

Make the width of the back at the natural waist 2 or 2½ inches, and extend the back line 1 to 1½ inch over the construction line at D.

When the straight line of the sidebody from 6 through 5 has been drawn, the skirt-seam can follow it for a full width skirt; but when a close skirt is preferred, reduce from D to R 2 inches and curve the seam from the waist down.

Locate the shoulder and armhole to measure; draw in two darts and separate the sidebodies.

The central lines, E to L and F to M, must reach down to the bottom.

Having figured out the amount of hip room needed, add it between U and V, and W and X, and run the seams equally on each side from the center line.

Transfer the two darts into one in the middle to be the size of one dart; take out 1 inch at side at 1, and reduce a trifle at V to hold a good curve.

The line from I to K is squared down by the waist line, but for such a long garment as this we draw another for the front from I to 1 inch forward of K. Add 2½ to 3 inches beyond the front-center line for a double-breasted front.

A broad collar like that shown on the collar plate, or a standing one, may be used.

Add full seams to this garment and ample cuffs to the sleeves, but do not make the latter quite so full at the top as for a jacket.

An opening may be left in the center of the back from C down.

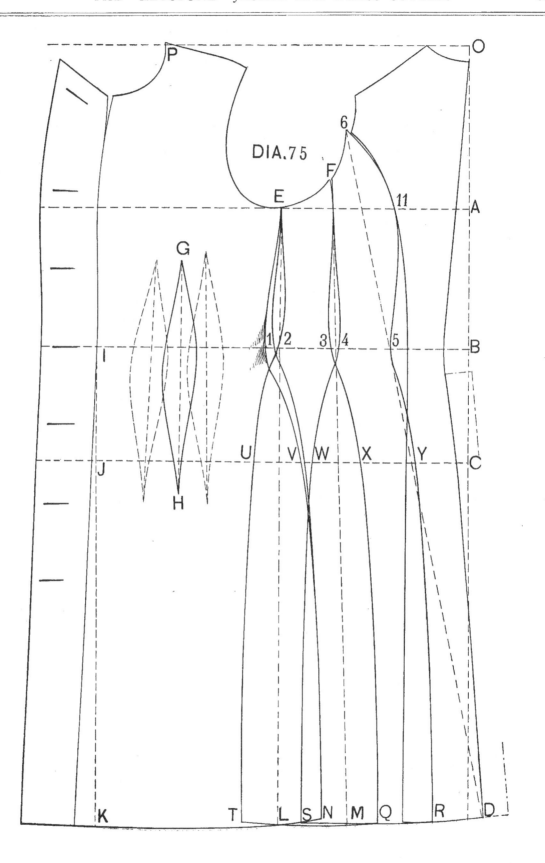

DRESS SKIRTS.

DIAGRAM 76.

IN drafting skirts the proportions of waist and hip should be carefully considered, for the darts that are taken out of the top of the skirt must be in accordance with the difference between the two sizes.

It is never necessary for an average form—one from 15 to 20 inches more in the hips than in the waist—to cut the darts more than 1 inch wide. In fact, it is advisable on forms that are flat in front to draw them ¾ inch and make the side darts which are over the prominent part of the hip 1 inch.

If there is more difference than 20 inches, then these darts must reach 1¼ inch at side. If the skirt is for a large person, who is corpulent, the darts both in front and at the side must be fully 1 inch wide.

In any case the system, as we lay it down, conforms to all shapes, and as will be seen, can be made to adapt itself to any size or style.

The seams can be located to suit the width of material, as we shall explain.

TO DRAFT.

First draw the line from O to B and C.

We will take for the waist measure 24, for the hip 40, and for the front length 40 inches.

Measure down from O to B, the waist, 24, and from B to C, the front length, 40.

Use point O as a pivot and sweep by it from B to H, and pivoting at the same point, sweep from C to define the bottom.

As the distance O C is longer than any tape measure, stick an awl into the table at O, tie a string to it long enough to reach to C, and then cast the sweep.

Place from B to 1 at the dart ¼ of waist, 3 inches. From 1 to 2—width of dart—is 1 inch. From 2 to 3 is ¼ waist, and from 3 to o—width of dart—is 1 inch. o to 4 is ¼ waist. *This gives 9 inches from B.*

From 4 to 5 we place 1¼ inch for the hip dart.

In the middle of each dart fix a point as D, E and F, and through these points from point o draw straight lines to the bottom.

Curve the darts 4½ inches down, as shown.

At a right angle with the line O F draw a line from F to G and place from 5 to G, 9 inches, which will be ample to make up the measure of waist and leave something for plaits.

At a right angle with the line 5 G draw a line down to U—the dotted line.

This line defines the closest skirt that can be made, but as it only hangs straight down, more room around the bottom will give it a better expression. We therefore add from U to K 12 inches and draw the line G K.

In gathering the size into the waist-band from G to 5, point G will be a trifle low to reach 5, so we raise the upper line 1 inch above G, and draw from 5 to this point, which is between G and 6.

This skirt hangs straight down all around except the plaiting formed in the back by the addition U to K.

To produce a skirt that will be very full, or will require a considerable amount of plaiting in the back, proceed as follows:

Locate point A in the middle between O and B, and draw a right-angled line which will reach L.

For this style the upper waist curve from F backward must be on the curve from 6 to 5.

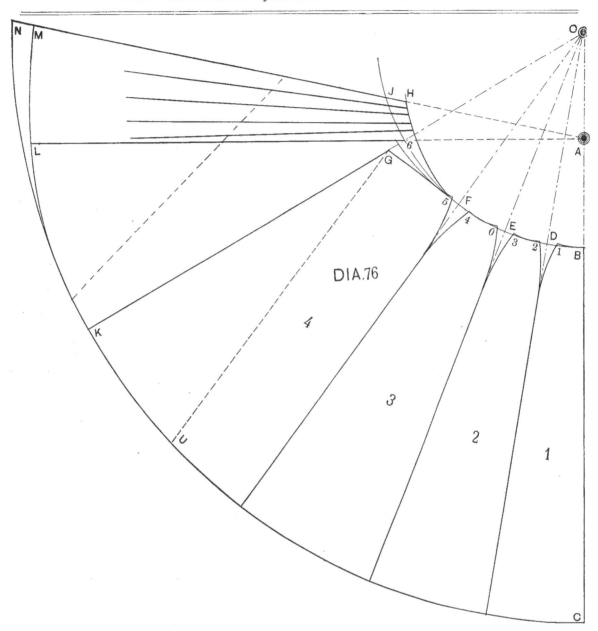

DIA. 76

The bottom remains the same as that of the first skirt. This is usually called the "Bell Skirt."

To give a skirt an extreme amount of fullness in the back, add from L to M 10 inches or more, and draw a line from A to M. The upper edge remains at H, but the lower is made 1½ to 2 inches longer at N, as shown.

The greater or lesser amount of fullness added produces the several different styles now made, the one just explained being called the "Umbrella."

On silks seams will have to be drawn on lines D, E and F, but no seam is put in from B to C. On woolen goods, where the width will permit, the first seam is on E line, and there is none at F. The darts must be cut in on all skirts.

The piece 3 and 4 is cut from cloth opened.

The very fullest may need a seam on the dotted diagonal line back of K.

THE FULL DRESS SKIRT.

DIAGRAM 77.

DRAFT as explained for Diagram 76, with the following exceptions:

Let the width X E be ⅓ waist.

Draw all the lines from O down. As this skirt is always made from narrow material it is, therefore, cut through the line.

From E to G add 12 to 18 inches, according to the width of plaiting desired.

This side gore, marked 5, is drawn with a curve from L to K.

Point L is ⅓ of the whole length from the waist down.

The train effect which we desire to produce requires that point K shall curve beyond the straight line Y from 12 to 20 inches, according to the train desired, and in order that it may fall on the floor ½ of the above, or 6 to 10 inches, is added to the length at K, below the first circle 6.

This edge must start from Z.

As the length of the line E L K increases, we are obliged to increase the length of the line of the back breadth, E L Y, to correspond, for the line E L K sews into the line E L Y.

In laying the lower edges together the sweep from Y to J must follow that of Z to K.

When point G is established draw a line through it from O to reach J.

The greater the curve from L to K the more the skirt will sweep back, but more length must be added at K and on the back piece.

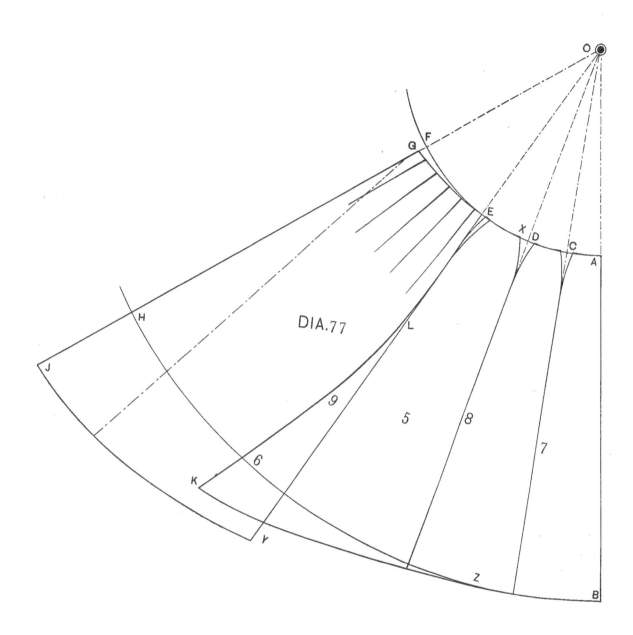

RIDING SKIRT.

THE FRONT.

DIAGRAM 78.—This diagram is laid out to and must be enlarged by inches. Draw lines O 4 and O G.

O to 1 is 5 inches.

From 1 to 4, the side length, is 43 inches.

From 1 to 2 is 3 inches.

O to A is 10 inches.

A to B is 3¾ inches.

B to C is ¾ inch.

C to D is 10¼ inches.

D to E is 5¼ inches.

E to F is 3½ inches.

F to G is 4½ inches.

From all of these points draw right-angled lines.

A to H is 6½ inches.

B to I is 4 inches.

C to J is 2 inches.

D to K is 7 inches.

E to L is 3¼ inches.

E to M is 13 inches.

F to N is 4½ inches.

G to P is 9 inches.

From 4 to 5 is 23½ inches.

From 4 to U is 48 inches.

U to T is 3 inches.

Draw a straight line P to T.

P to R is 15 inches.

R to S is 1¾ inch.

The line H 5 is the center of the front, and from 2 to 4 is the left side.

At 3 there is a cut, 7 inches long, which is made up to button.

Point M is the top of the knee.

This diagram must be cut on the right side of the goods.

DIA. 78

THE BACK.

DIAGRAM 79.—Draw the lines O F and O E.

O to A is 2¾ inches.

A to B is 4¼ inches.

B to C is 1½ inch.

C to D is 6¼ inches.

J to E is the same length as from 2 to 4 on Diagram 78.

O to F is 15 inches.

A to G is 12 inches.

B to H is 7 inches.

C to J is 1¼ inch.

D to K is 18 inches.

E, across the bottom, to P is 39 inches.

P down to lower edge is 1¼ inch.

Up from P to X is the same length as T to P on the front.

X to Q is 3½ inches.

X to L is 3 inches.

L to M is 1¾ inch.

M to N is 2¼ inches.

Q to R is 9½ inches.

X to S is 3 inches.

L to T is 7¼ inches.

T to U is 2½ inches.

M to V is 12¾ inches.

N to W is 8 inches.

Now form the outlines.

VW is under the knee, K is the seat, and the side J E is the left side.

Sew up U T and then V S to R.

F to P will now sew to C P T of the front.

Sometimes a band is sewn to the waist, but generally the waist is only taped.

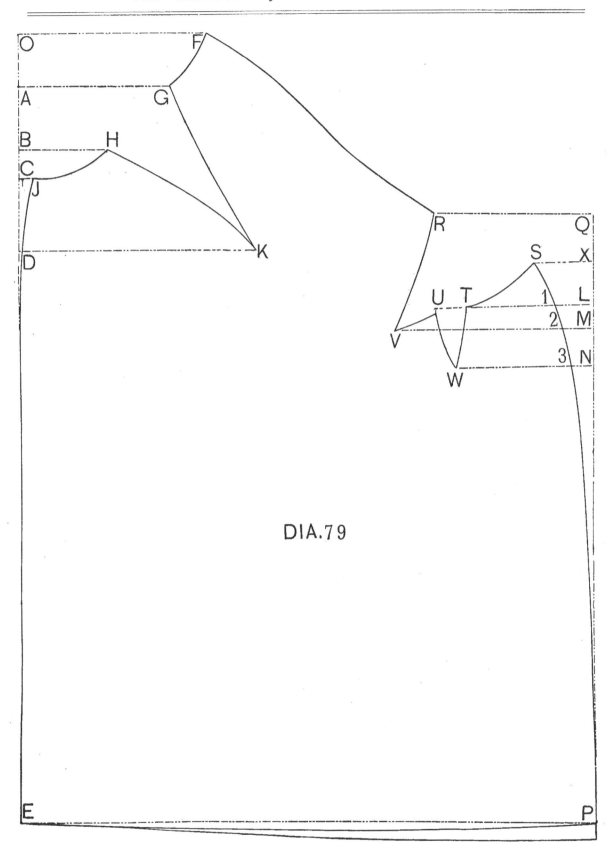

DIA. 79

TROUSERS.

DIAGRAM 80.

THE FOREPART.—The measures are as follows: Rise 10, Side length 30, Waist 25, Seat 40, Knee 18 and Bottom 17.

Draw line A E, and place from A to C the rise 10 inches.

A to E is the outside length from the waist to the heel.

D is half-way between C and E.

Draw the cross lines.

C to O is ⅓ seat, and O to J is the same.

In the middle between O and J is F.

Square up from F.

N to Z is ½ and ⅛ waist, and the ⅛ is to be taken out as a V between T and U

Curve from Z to C.

In the middle between A and C draw line B.

E to 5 is ⅙ seat.

Draw the center line from O to 5.

The bottom 6 to L is 7½ inches.

G to 1 is ¼ knee, 4½ inches, and G to 2 is the same.

Connect J with 1 and 1 with L and finish the side-seam.

THE BACKPART.—J to K is 1¼ inch.

From 6 to 4 is ½ bottom and ½ inch, and L to outside-seam is the same

Point 3 is ½ inch from 1, and D is ½ inch from 2.

Draw a line from C to I and square up from I to M by point C.

T to M is ¼ seat.

M to Q is ¼ waist plus ⅛ and 2 inches for seams.   The ⅛ is to govern the width of the V at X Y.

B to R is 3½ inches.

Shape the outlines.

The opening is on the side.

In measuring let the lady sit in a chair and take the length from the waist to the chair.   Then ask her to stand and take the outside length to the heel.

The waist and seat sizes are taken close.

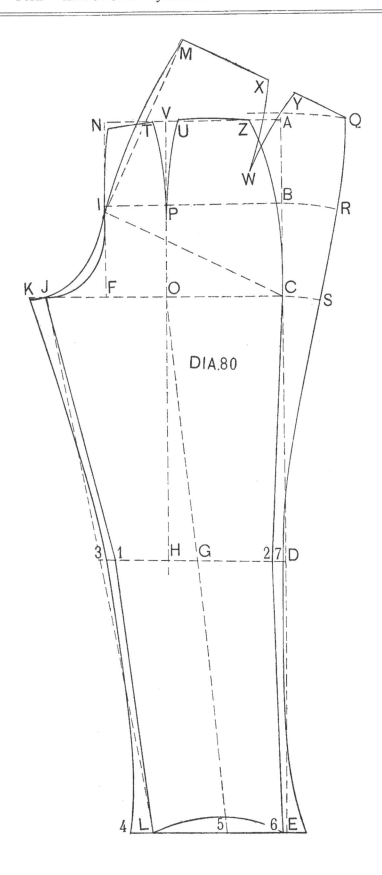

BREECHES.

DIAGRAM 81.

THE measures are the same as for Diagram 80.

In drafting the rise is the same and the sizes and divisions are placed in the same manner as already explained to obtain the points.

Go down from O to N, an average of 7 inches.

From N to dot is 1 inch.

Draw a line from O through the unlettered dot.

O to G is 14; to H 16, and to the bottom I, is 20 inches.

From 1 to F is 2 inches.

F to M is 7 inches.

G to D is 3½ inches.

G to K is 4 inches.

F to 4 is 2 inches.

The back-seams at knee are ½ inch outside of the front-seams.

The seat line is drawn as before at a right angle with S C; point W is located ¼ waist above Q, and the waist size is applied from W to Z as already explained.

The outlines are now drawn as shown.

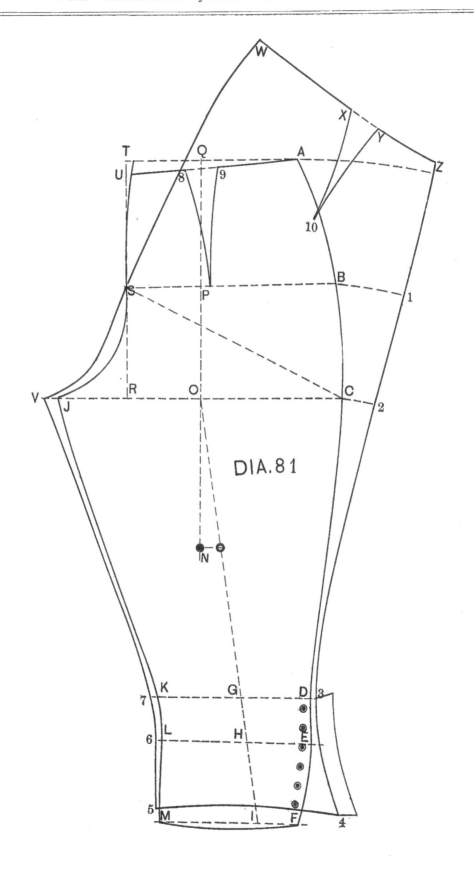

DIA. 81

Illustrations from
The Delineator
June, 1895 and June, 1896

Ladies' Jacket. Tan coating and dark brown velvet were the fabric choices recommended for this well-fitted jacket. The wide sleeves are typical of 1895 and could be made with the "Very Full Sleeve" pattern *Keystone* provided. The comparatively small collar trimmed with velvet is also a common feature of women's suits of the era.

Ladies' Outdoor Toilette. An example of a lavish Eton jacket paired with a shirtwaist. Recommended for the promenade, this design was fashioned from dark green fabric and black moiré, with an off-white taffeta waist. The front panels of this Eton were designed never quite to meet.

Ladies' Puritan Cape. Dark violet fabric was recommended for this cape, called a "Puritan Cape" because of its "rather severe outline." Basically a circle cut out of cloth (like the "Three-Quarter Cape" *Keystone* provided), it was interlined with stiff crinoline, and featured ostrich feathers and ribbon. "The simplicity and excellent style of this cape will be appreciated by conservative women," wrote the editors of *The Delineator*.

Ladies' Double-Breasted Jacket. A popular style for women in the 1890s, this double-breasted jacket was made of "tobacco-brown" serge. The roll collar, enormous sleeves, and hip length were all fashionable in 1895.

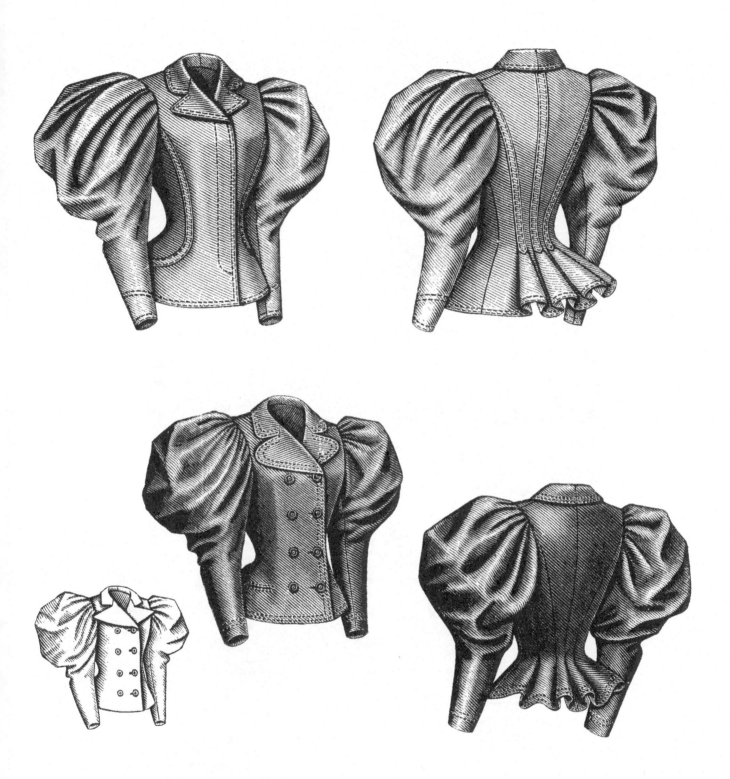

A Variety of Jackets Popular in the 1890s. Peplums (called "skirts" by *Keystone*) were popular in 1895, for carefully pleated peplums offered a tailored, but feminine look. Other jackets were cut so carefully that the backs were full, yet neither pleated nor gathered. Shorter Eton jackets didn't button in front, and often featured wider collars. Large sleeves predominated throughout, which explains why *Keystone* offers several patterns for wide sleeves.

Jackets (cont.)

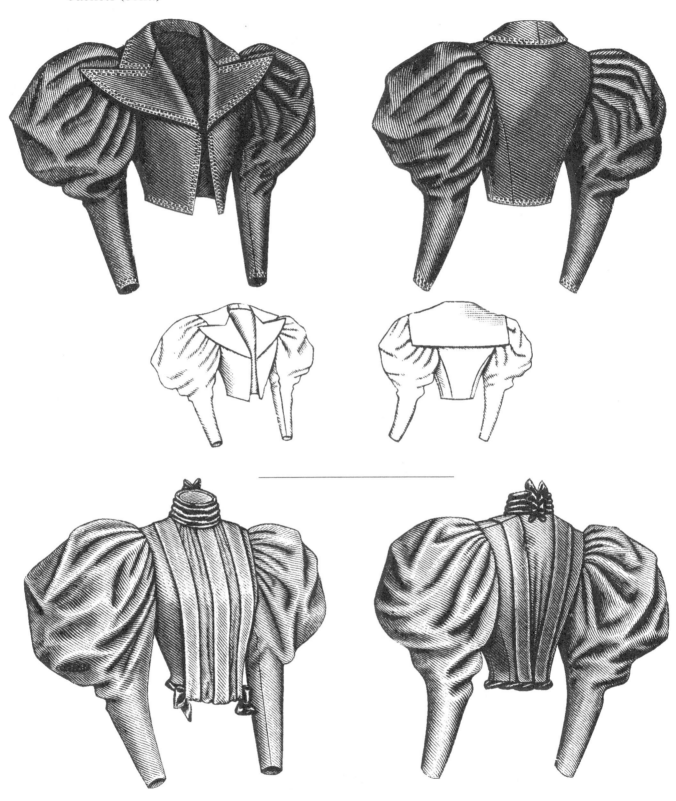

Ladies' Box-Plaited Basque Waist (two lower illustrations). The shirtwaist was fast becoming *the* important garment every woman needed. Its versatility was renowned, and the basic pattern *Keystone* provided could easily be altered to achieve a vast array of variations. This shirtwaist, with box pleats, high collar, and full sleeves, is typical.Ä

Ladies' Outdoor Toilette. Box coats were a newly revived trend, and with their large sleeves and loose fit, seem almost out of place amid the snug-fitting designs of the era. The skirt is rounded and gored, just as noted in *Keystone*'s description. The entire "thoroughly practical" outfit is recommended for shopping.

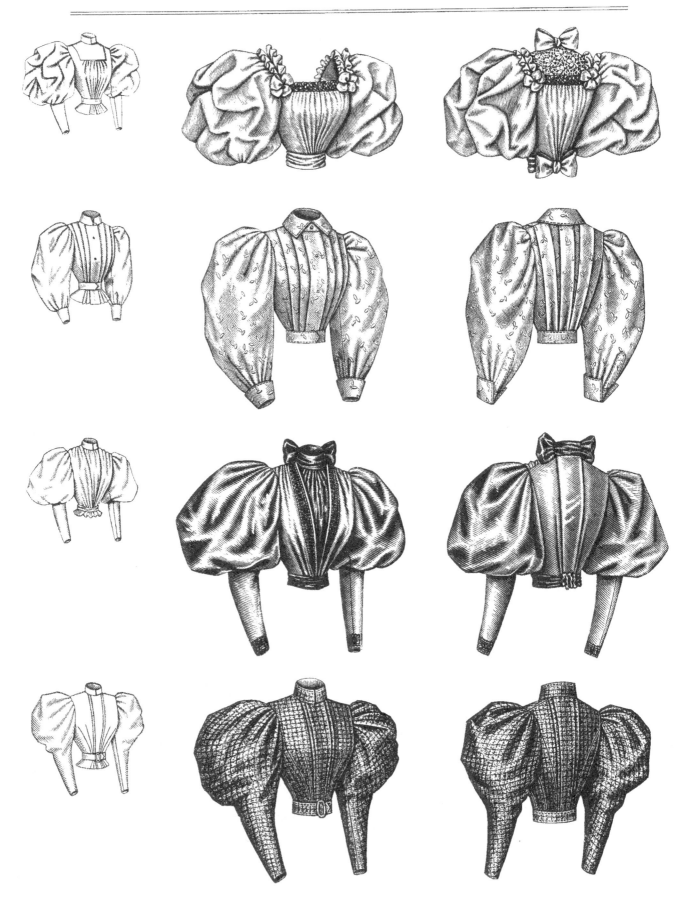

Typical, Fashionable Shirtwaists of 1895. Each shirtwaist required almost
six yards of cloth, and featured massive sleeves, stiff high collars, and box pleating.

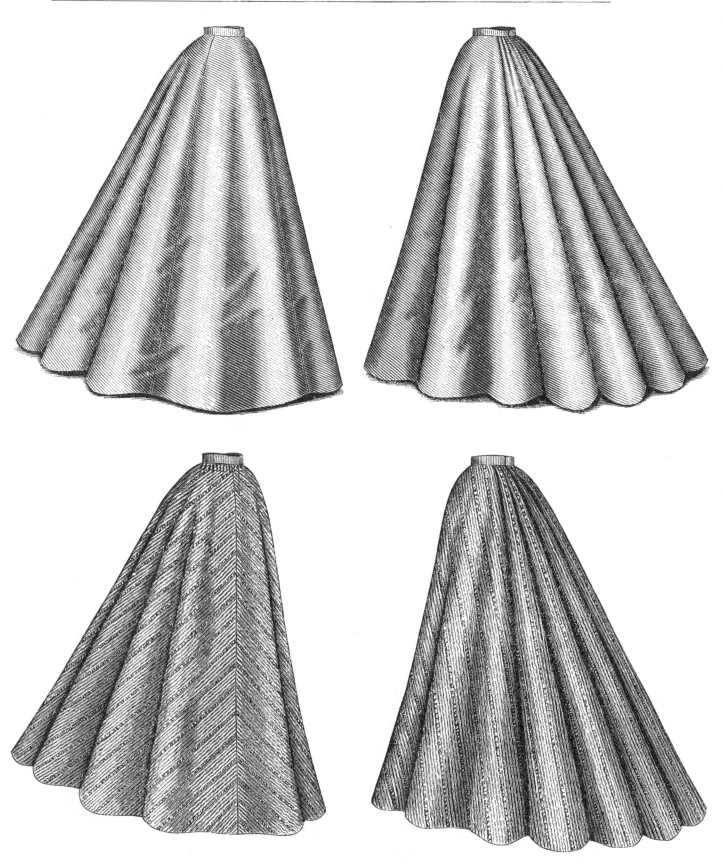

Typical Skirts of 1895. Full and circular, these skirts are very simple, with just a touch of interest at the back, where a little gathering accentuated the derriere, and a slightly lengthened back hem lightly swept the streets.

Combination for a Ladies' Costume. A common style of ladies' suit, featuring a circular skirt, vest, and jacket. A tailor with *Keystone* at his side, could easily recreate this fashion plate.

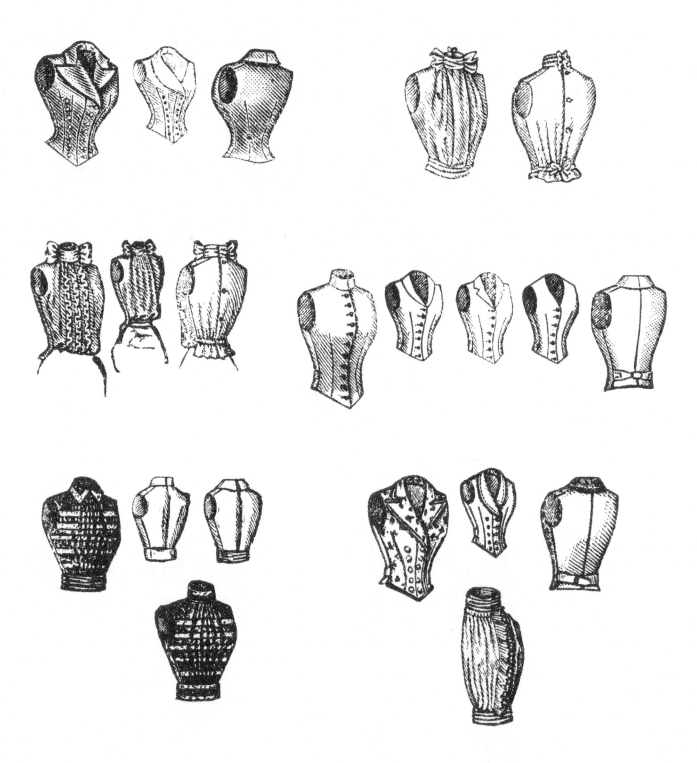

Ladies' Vests. Ladies' vests mimicked men's, but added feminine detailing. The fronts were typically pointed, and small or wide collars were common. In the back, cinches for a snug waist were sometimes found, but the entire garment was always tightly fitted with darts, seaming, and tiny buttons.

Two Typical Ladies' Suits of the Mid-1890s. Both suits feature "mannish" woolen cloth, fabric-hogging sleeves, circular skirts, peplums, and snugly fitted waists—all style elements accounted for in *Keystone*. "For the promenade, whether in the morning or afternoon, a tailor-made suit is always in perfect taste," opined the editors of *The Delineator*.

Ladies Toilette. Considered appropriate for outings, this brown cloth jacket is closely fitted in back and at the sides, with huge leg-o-mutton sleeves and tidy little pockets.

Two Jackets Typical of the Mid-1890s. The open-fronted blazer is made from blue-and-white serge and is coupled with a printed white shirtwaist. The woolen single-breasted jacket is designed to be worn on slightly more formal occasions, and is trimmed with white lapels and cuffs.

Double-Breasted Ladies' Suit. A typical suit with a wide
peplum and plenty of machine-stitched topstitching.

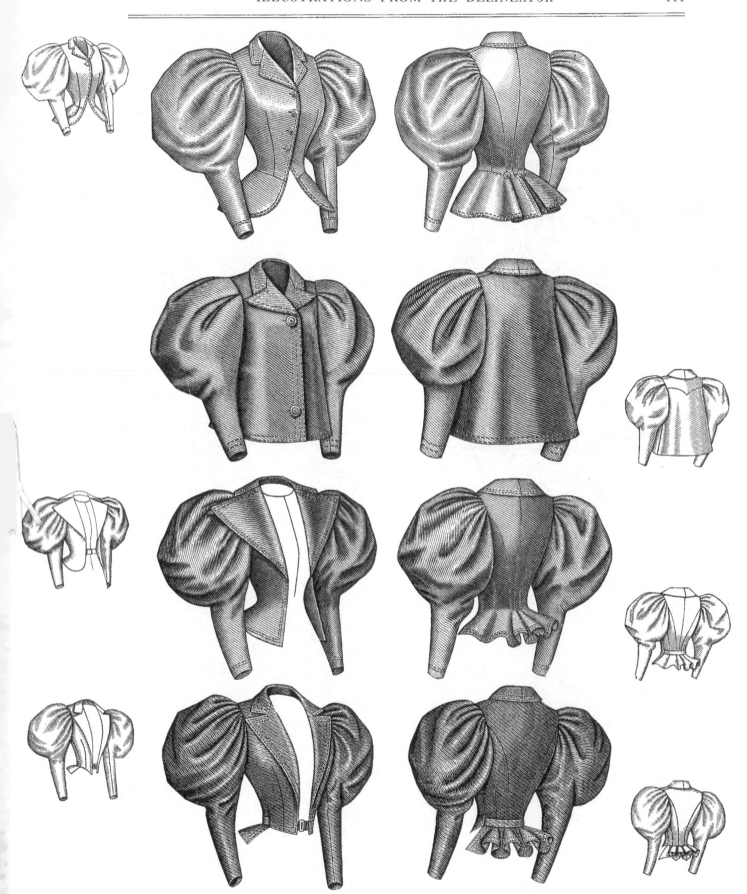

A Variety of Jacket Styles. A selection of jackets featured in *The Delineator*,
including a cutaway, blazer, saque (box coat), and Eton jacket.U

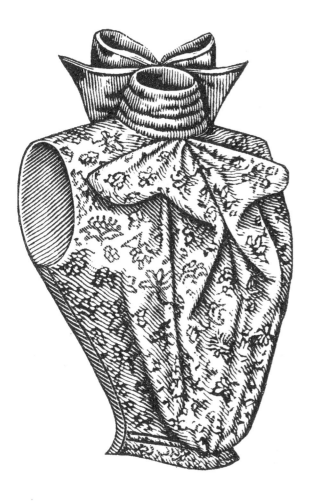

Front View.

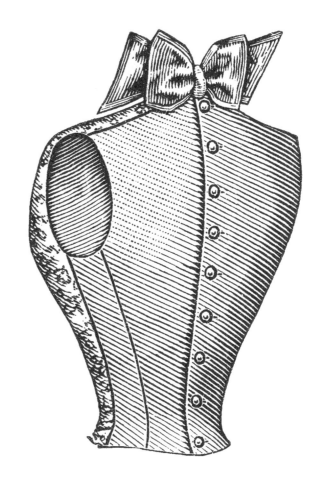

Back View.

Ladies' Vest. "This attractive vest may be worn with blazers, and other jackets," suggested the editors of *The Delineator*, recommending silk as an appropriate fabric. Tailors using *Keystone* could easily recreate this style.